# RAF's Centenary Flypast

# RAF's Centenary Flypast

The Story Behind the Event that Marked
100 Years of the Royal Air Force

Wing Commander Kevin Gatland OBE, MA, RAF

Foreword by Air Chief Marshal Sir Stephen Hillier GCB, CBE, DFC, MA, RAF

AIR WORLD

**AIR WORLD**

## RAF'S CENTENARY FLYPAST
### The Story Behind the Event that Marked 100 Years of the Royal Air Force

First published in Great Britain in 2021 by
Air World
An imprint of
Pen & Sword Books Ltd
Yorkshire – Philadelphia

ISBN 978 1 52678 840 5

Printed and bound in India by Replika Press Pvt. Ltd.
Typeset in Ehrhardt MT Std 11.5/14 by
SJmagic DESIGN SERVICES, India.

Pen & Sword Books Ltd incorporates the imprints of Pen & Sword Archaeology, Air World Books, Atlas, Aviation, Battleground, Discovery, Family History, History, Maritime, Military, Naval, Politics, Social History, Transport, True Crime, Claymore Press, Frontline Books, Praetorian Press, Seaforth Publishing and White Owl

For a complete list of Pen & Sword titles please contact

PEN & SWORD BOOKS LIMITED
47 Church Street, Barnsley, South Yorkshire, S70 2AS, England
E-mail: enquiries@pen-and-sword.co.uk
Website: www.pen-and-sword.co.uk

Or
PEN AND SWORD BOOKS
1950 Lawrence Rd, Havertown, PA 19083, USA
E-mail: Uspen-and-sword@casematepublishers.com
Website: www.penandswordbooks.com

Contains public sector information licensed under the Open Government Licence v3.0 and imagery licenced from the Ministry of Defence.

Thanks also to the CAA/NATS, Mr Andy Chase, Mr Tim O'Brien and Squadron Prints for their kind permissions to reproduce their imagery, charts and photography.

# Contents

# Foreword
## Air Chief Marshal Sir Stephen Hillier GCB, CBE, DFC, MA, RAF

If truly historic moments can be defined by remembering where you were at the time, then the RAF100 Flypast on 10 July 2018 surely makes that mark. For long after that memorable day, people from every walk of life – few with any previous connection with the Royal Air Force – would tell me just where they saw perhaps the most striking moment of our Centenary year.

I certainly remember where I was that day: standing on a dais on the forecourt of Buckingham Palace, in front of over a thousand members of the Royal Air Force, parading for Her Majesty the Queen and the Royal Family. As the successive waves of the flypast aircraft came into view over the Mall, I could not have felt greater pride in the skill, precision and professionalism of the RAF. It seemed clear that the nation felt the same way too, from the roars of approval from the crowds which filled the Mall and the surrounding parks, to the people and traffic at a standstill on roads, bridges and the tops of buildings on the flypast route, to the millions watching live on television in the UK and around the world. It was indeed the signature moment of RAF100, one which captured the nation's attention.

Success on that day did not happen by chance, but reflected an immense amount of hard work over many months by many people already busy with one of the most demanding periods of sustained UK and overseas operational activity which the RAF had experienced for generations. It was an immense team effort, requiring the complete range of RAF specialist skills and capabilities – across the whole Force, everyone had a vital role in delivering the flypast, and can be immensely proud of what they achieved.

But perhaps above all else, the RAF100 Flypast was a demonstration of superb planning, organisation and command and control. I am therefore delighted that Wing Commander Kevin Gatland has chosen to write this most valuable record of the conception, planning and delivery of the flypast, because more than any other one person, it was he who owned the flypast from start to finish. I am equally delighted that his exceptional efforts were fittingly recognised by the award of an OBE in 2019.

The goals of RAF100 were to Commemorate our rich heritage, to Celebrate the RAF of today, and to Inspire future generations. The RAF100 Flypast convincingly touched on all of these goals, in a way which was truly historic and which leave us a proud, strong and lasting legacy. This important book will reinforce that legacy and will ensure that the flypast lives long in the memory of everyone who was a part of it, and those who witnessed this headline moment of the history of the Royal Air Force.

*Air Chief Marshal Sir Stephen Hillier*
*GCB, CBE, DFC, MA, RAF*

# Prologue

On 1 April 2018, the Royal Air Force, the world's first independent Air Force, turned 100. Celebrating the Centenary was a national event with numerous events staged up and down the country. The most striking was the massed parade and flypast down the Mall in front of Buckingham Palace.

In the presence of Her Majesty the Queen, one thousand Royal Air Force personnel marched on parade, while overhead flew a flypast of epic proportions. One hundred and three aircraft, representing the vast array of Royal Air Force military capability flew down the Mall starting at exactly 1300 hrs. To Commemorate, Celebrate and Inspire, the day's events formed part of Royal Air Force history.

One thousand Royal Air Force personnel marched on parade for Her Majesty the Queen on 10 July 2018 to mark the centenary birthday of the world's first independent air force. (© *Crown Copyright 2018, WO Andy Malthouse*)

This book lets you in on the behind-the-scenes actions that brought the flypast to its majestic conclusion. Detailing the flypast's initial conception, planning and managing the 'What Ifs?', it brings to life the challenges behind the event.

*Wing Commander Kevin Gatland OBE*
*April 2020*

© *Crown Copyright 2018*

# List of Participating Squadrons and Units

| | |
|---|---|
| *Vortex* | 28 (AC) Squadron, 33 Squadron, 230 Squadron, RAF Benson; 7 Squadron, 18 Squadron and 27 Squadron, RAF Odiham |
| *Spectre* | 202 Squadron, 60 Squadron, Central Flying School, RAF Shawbury |
| *Dakota* | Battle of Britain Memorial Flight, RAF Coningsby |
| *Memorial* | Battle of Britain Memorial Flight, RAF Coningsby |
| *Warboys* | 16 Squadron, No 3 Flying Training School, RAF Cranwell |
| *Swift* | 72(R) Squadron, RAF Linton-On-Ouse |
| *Snake* | 14 Squadron, RAF Waddington |
| *Zorro* | 47 Squadron, RAF Brize Norton |
| *Grizzly* | XXIV Squadron, RAF Brize Norton |
| *Blackcat* | 99 Squadron, RAF Brize Norton and 32 Squadron, RAF Northolt |
| *Snapshot* | 5(AC) Squadron, RAF Waddington |
| *Tartan* | 10 Squadron, 101 Squadron, RAF Brize Norton |
| *Goose* | 51 Squadron, RAF Waddington |
| *Sentry* | 8 Squadron, RAF Waddington |
| *Aggressor* | 100 Squadron, RAF Leeming |
| *Ninja* | IV Squadron, RAF Valley |
| *Monster* | IX(B) Squadron, 31 Squadron, RAF Marham |
| *Gibson* | 617 Squadron, RAF Marham |
| *Typhoon* | 1(F) Squadron, 2(AC) Squadron, 6 Squadron, RAF Lossiemouth; 3(F) Squadron, 11 Squadron, 29(R) Squadron, RAF Coningsby |
| *Red Arrows* | Royal Air Force Aerobatic Team, RAF Scampton |
| *RAF(U)* | Swanwick |

## Chapter 1

# Introduction

The flypast was nearly here. The time was approaching 1200 Zulu (1300 hrs Local time). This was the culmination of well over a year's worth of work. The slight pit of apprehension in my stomach had now disappeared, only to have moved upwards to be a lump in my throat. Our biggest threat, the weather, had been kind and the layer of high, but thin, white clouds and slight breeze meant that the worries over the weather on the day had been negated some hours earlier. We had taken the morning weather brief and reviewed the situation over the whole route, including all of the departure and recovery airfields that the flypast aircraft would be using. It was satisfactory. The summer had been hot so far. Really hot. This cloud cover, gentle breeze and cooler temperature of twenty-two degrees was a welcome respite for the one thousand Royal Air Force personnel who would be marching in full dress uniform from Horse Guards Parade, down the Mall to Buckingham Palace in the minutes prior to the flypast appearing overhead. The day, featuring a Guard of Honour, the seven Royal Air Force Queen's Colours, fifty-five Squadron Standards and four Escort Squadrons showed the Royal Air Force was very much on parade. Up in the skies, the airborne visibility was remarkably good. Very often in UK summertime, the visibility can decrease quite markedly after such a long spell of warm weather, but today was near-on perfect. You could see for miles. All pertinent airfields had reported good serviceability status and the aircraft were all airborne and had been busy forming up in their holding patterns over the sea and land and were now flying inbound to Central London in loose formations, tightening up once they came within about 30 miles of Buckingham Palace. Flying in close formation can be tiring and we wanted the very best to be displayed for Her Majesty the Queen and the public. The media coverage had been impressive thus far, we had done interviews, both for TV and radio as well as numerous written pieces which had hit the various printed outlets. Social media had been heavily used with the content being liked, commented on and shared over one million times. Today, the BBC were dedicating live coverage of the whole event, broadcast across the globe and we had both a BBC and Sky News helicopter airborne filming the event. The scale of airspace used was the largest the Civil Aviation Authority had ever had to issue, and thanks to the very close collaboration and agreements with London Heathrow and London City airports over the previous year, we had a plan which integrated as best we could with the huge volume of commercial airliner traffic which needed to take off and land from these very busy airports.

The whole plan was built around the management of risk, employing mitigation tactics where we could. The flypast plan had been built and briefed, but with geographically dispersed aircraft departure locations we needed a centralised command cell to manage the flypast on the day. I went down to London the night before, 9 July. I wanted to further remove another risk which could cause problems, namely transporting myself from my home into Central London. The last thing that was needed after all this planning was a delayed or cancelled train or other random issue causing me to be late. Besides, the morning would be busy enough ensuring all the elements of the plan came together for a 'Go' decision to be made.

Arriving early at New Zealand House, I passed through security at the front door and got into the elevator. Pressing the button for the top floor my mind ran through the sequence of events we needed to enable the flypast to get this critical 'Go' decision. Weather, aircraft, airfields, air traffic, security. Our hosts, the air staff in the New Zealand Embassy, met us at the top and I found a quiet corner of the large open-plan room to base myself for the day. There would be many people arriving, ranging from the hierarchy of the Royal Air Force to industry partners and their guests and I wanted to have an area that was out of the way. Setting up the laptop and opening up the document which contained my complete checklist of all of the things that I would need, signalled the start of the day. I reported directly to Air Vice Marshal Gerry Mayhew, the Air Officer Commanding Number 1 Group, but today he was also the Senior Responsible Officer (SRO) for the RAF 100 Flypast. It was to him I would pass all of the information gleaned, and he who would ultimately give the 'Go' decision.

From our command cell in New Zealand House the morning was spent busily collating all of the Go / No Go criteria of the flypast as well as gaining a full understanding of how many serviceable aircraft we had airborne, including the spare aircraft just in case an aircraft could not complete the flypast and had to turn back. A full weather brief from the Met Office gave us confidence that the criteria for conducting a safe flypast would be met. We have very strict regulations for the conduct of flypasts and one of those rules required aircraft to have a minimum of 5 kilometres visibility, be 500ft vertically clear of cloud and stay 1,500 metres horizontally clear of cloud. We therefore needed a minimum cloud-base of 1,700ft over Central London and 1,800ft on the egress routes. If we had all of this, the full flypast could take place. The greatest concern was always for the cloud-base. If the weather did not meet these criteria, we did have a few back-up options available; using the slower aircraft such as the helicopters, for example, as their weather limits were less restrictive.

Our first decision point was scheduled for 0930Z / 1030 local time. This followed the weather brief and would allow us the option to stop any aircraft needlessly getting airborne if it was obvious that the weather would be unfit for the flypast later on. The slides from the Met Office had been sent through to my laptop as well as to two separate mobile phones – a back-up in case something didn't quite work, or the laptop didn't receive the email for whatever reason. No chances could be taken. We scanned the slides and with a rather large sigh of relief saw that there didn't appear to be anything significant that could affect the chances of a full flypast. The forecast predicted slightly poorer conditions over in one of our main holding areas near Southwold with various layers of cloud between 1,500ft to 5,000ft, although none of it was particularly thick. The subsequent phone call with the Met Office confirmed all of this but also gave us confidence that the crews should not struggle to get their formations through it. Pleasingly, the forecast weather conditions over Central London gave us 25 kilometres visibility and a scattered to broken cloud-base at 4,500ft. This was more than sufficient for what we needed. I put the phone down and formally requested the Air Vice Marshal's approval for a 'Continue' decision. It was given. Aircraft would start getting airborne shortly. The approval set in motion the subsequent sequence of events. For us in London, this mostly meant continuing to monitor the weather, aircraft and airfield serviceability as well as any security updates. A change to any of these may mean a change to our expected plan. A single weather brief early in the morning however, was not sufficient to give us the full confidence required that all would be well with the flypast. Weather changes, sometimes quite rapidly, and forecasts can be wrong. We could not take that risk. Flying the planned one hundred aircraft flypast into poor weather while in very tight close formations could be catastrophic – we had to be sure it would be good enough. The decision of launching additional 'weather-ship' aircraft to back up the weather forecast had been made some months previous and had long been standard practice for the annual Queen's Birthday Flypasts. These dedicated aircraft would provide a pilot's eye view and give us the exact cloud-base and a very good estimate of visibility with which to compare against the weather brief from the Met Office. At 1030Z (1130L), two-and-a-half hours before the flypast was due over the Palace, two Hawk fast-jet aircraft launched to trace the ingress routes into Central London as well as the holds and egress routes that the aircraft would have to fly post the Palace. Their PiReps, or Pilot Reports, on the weather would be critical to the main Go / No Go decision point scheduled for 1125Z (1225L). If they reported lower than the required cloud-bases or poor visibility, the options would be to cancel the whole thing or utilise one of the three alternate weather plans we had available. The timing for those aircraft to get the message to us was critical. Shortly after the decision point time of 1125Z, aircraft would start leaving their holds and running inbound and that was not a good time to start changing the plan! It was a balance between leaving it as late as possible to get the most accurate weather reports we could versus relaying the amendment instructions to all of the crews via Air Traffic Control. With forty minutes to go, at 1120Z (1220L), all of the weather reports from the pilots were in. While we could see from our vantage point in London that the weather was perfect here for the flypast, we had to rely on these weather reports as well as reports from airfields on the route to complete the picture. All reports noted that the weather was good and the hold areas were even slightly better than previously expected. Unfortunately, our London weather-ship helicopter, from 32 Squadron, Royal Flight, was not able to be present, having suffered a cracked windscreen from a bird-strike a few days previous. Thankfully, the back-up option of using the NPAS Police helicopter as our weather-ship worked well. Although we could see the weather was fit, his confirmation was very welcome. The Police helicopter also played an important secondary role. We would normally place an RAF photographer on-board the 32 Squadron helicopter to get some pictures from above the flypast. We managed to switch the photographer into the Police helicopter to do this. From our vantage point, we could see the Police helicopter was now stationed in the overshoot of the Palace – the best place to get the pictures.

The good weather also meant that we would have a little more flexibility on the serviceability of the airfields, predominately for aircraft recovering after the flypast. Poor weather at the airfield would mean aircraft having to conduct instrument approaches rather than the more usual visual approaches. These took far more time, meant more work for Air Traffic Control and additionally complicated getting the mass of aircraft back on the ground. This was particularly pertinent for our largest formation of the day – the twenty-two Typhoon aircraft which would need to be sequenced to land back at RAF Coningsby.

Just before 1125Z (1225L), the final run through of all of the decision matrix was in full flow. The picture was 'clean' from my contact working in the security sector. We had no concerns from the weather, all of the airfields were reporting either perfect serviceability or at least sufficient for the day and we now knew all of the aircraft were in place. Squadron Leader Dunc Hewat, the liaison officer based at our master Air Traffic Control hub at Swanwick confirmed that they reported no concerns. Everything was on track.

Despite our long-held concerns about getting a full complement of one hundred aircraft for the flypast, we actually had in excess of that available. As part of the contingency planning we had strategically located a number of additional aircraft across some of the formations which acted as airborne spares. We had spare helicopters, Tornado GR4s, Typhoons and a C-130 Hercules. As part of the practice scenarios, airborne spares had been fully briefed to take up empty positions should other elements across their formation not be present. The additional C-130, for example, would, if needed, fit in immediately behind the single C-130 already in the flypast. In addition, we had also provisioned for an option for the two spare GR4s to take up positions either within the F-35 Lightning formation or immediately behind the main Tornado formation. The benefit of these options is that it would give us additional flexibility should we be short of the planned one hundred aircraft for the day. Now, despite having spent months wondering whether we would be just short of the one hundred aircraft, it turned out to not be a factor. Instead we had the very opposite and were gifted an opportunity to exceed it. At 1125Z, the overall decision from

Air Vice Marshal Mayhew was made. It was a 'Go'. But as a slight twist, the additional C-130 and two Tornado aircraft were also given permission to join the main formation. We were on for one hundred and three aircraft.

So, this was it – on 10 July 2018, one hundred years and one hundred days after the formation of the world's first independent air force, the largest flypast in a generation was beginning. I've been asked why the extra one hundred days – why not celebrate on 1 April since the Royal Air Force was formed on 1 April 1918 following the merger of the Army's Royal Flying Corps and the Navy's Royal Naval Air Service? There happened to be a range of factors. 1 April 2018 was Easter Sunday, and there were obviously a variety of issues with using that day. There was also a desire to have as many international air force chiefs and senior attendees as possible. A number of other high profile and important military aviation events were also happening later in the year in July, so obtaining their attendance in the UK over two events separated by just three months may have limited attendance. The 10 July immediately preceded many of these other military events (such as the RIAT airshow) and the day also marked the anniversary of the official start date of the Battle of Britain. Finally, the weather in the UK in April is typically wetter, windier and cloudier than in July. With all these factors, a decision was made some months earlier that one hundred days after the 1 April would be the celebration day – 10 July. From a flypast and parade perspective, with the summer sun, warmer temperatures and high cloud-base, it certainly turned out to be a well-made decision.

At just a total of nine minutes and fifteen seconds in duration, it seemed somewhat surreal that such a short period of time had taken so many months to coordinate and plan. In the distance, from the balcony atop our vantage point of New Zealand House, which stands just opposite Horse Guards Parade, the first dots of the lead aircraft, the Pumas and Chinnoks, labelled with the Air Traffic Control callsign, *Vortex* started to slowly come into view. Travelling at 90 knots groundspeed, about 105 mph, they flew, silently to us at first but then, as they came closer the rhythmic beating of the rotor blades could be heard churning up the air as they approached. It seemed an agonising amount of time and while I had complete confidence that they would make their time over the Palace to the second, it still didn't stop me worrying. Gazing across London I took in the sight. The public were out in their thousands – having done a couple of Queen's Birthday Flypasts previously, I knew there would be people out to see but I was genuinely amazed at the scale. The Mall was full, the bridges were packed, Trafalgar Square had come to a complete standstill, people were on the roofs and about ten minutes earlier office workers had flooded out of the buildings in the immediate vicinity to watch the spectacle. Although we couldn't see directly into the Mall, as it was obscured by trees and buildings, the live BBC coverage was being played via an iPad sat on a table, and it showed the Mall completely full of people. This truly was a once in a lifetime event. It was the third biggest flypast the RAF had ever put together under Her Majesty the Queen. The largest was on 15 July 1953 for the Queen's Coronation Review at RAF Odiham where 641 aircraft participated. The second largest was in 1990 where 168 aircraft participated in the 50th anniversary of the Battle of Britain. And now there was this one. And we had made sure it would be a good one.

As the first and second formations of helicopters, callsigns *Vortex* and *Spectre*, thundered down the Mall and passed over Buckingham Palace they started their hard left turn. This cleared the way for the faster Battle of Britain Memorial Flight aircraft, the familiar sound of their Merlin engines could be heard. It was an incredible noise and one that would have brought a sense of relief during the dark days of the Blitz during the Second World War to the citizens of London knowing that the RAF were up defending with all their might against the scourge of the German Luftwaffe bombers. They gracefully crossed, much to the delight of the watching crowds. Thirty seconds behind were the Prefect and Tucano training aircraft formations; the Prefect being one of the latest additions to the RAF and Tucano due, over the next couple of years, to go out of service. Next followed the Shadow aircraft and then the heavy aircraft with the venerable and longest serving platform, the Hercules, with the Atlas, C17, BAe 146, Sentinel, Voyager, Rivet Joint and the E-3D Sentry spaced behind. It was a shame that we could spare so few of these aircraft to put into the flypast, but all were high value assets in very short supply. Frankly, we were lucky we got what we did.

The large arrow formation of Hawk T1 aircraft from 100 Squadron at RAF Leeming marked the start of the fast jet formation pieces. These had been practised over the preceding few weeks and I just hoped that all the formations looked tight to those viewing from the Mall. Hawk T2s followed in a diamond 9, leading Tornado GR4 and F-35 Lightning aircraft. The iconic centrepiece was next to come. Kept close-hold until the day, I could hear the crowd's applause and admiration of the twenty-two Typhoon fighters as they perfectly formed the '100' in the sky. Despite being a Tornado man through and through, this sight and sound was incredible. I doubt I'll ever hear forty-four EJ200 engines in synchronous roar again. As they swept past, the final formation, the Red Arrows with their world famous iconic red Hawk T1 aircraft trailing red, white and blue smoke concluded the event. I stood for a moment staring out above the London skyline watching them disappear, unable to gather any words; it certainly made for a climactic end to the flypast. But while the public saw the final formation fly over, the engine noise fade and coloured smoke disappear, there was still much work to be done and the crews had just entered one of the most challenging phases of the flypast. This was the closest that all of the aircraft had been during the day. With just thirty seconds between each formation, each holding a plus or minus five second tolerance against their allocated timing, the task now was to safely deconflict them apart, not just from the other formations, but also from within their own formation. Deconflicting over one hundred aircraft during this phase had meant a huge amount of the planning effort had gone into making it safe and therefore a success. The flypast was not over until every single aircraft had landed safely and that would take at least another hour.

The graceful simplicity of tight formations of aircraft just thirty seconds apart over Buckingham Palace hid a complex, multi-faceted and intricately coordinated plan. From the thousand-plus engineers who directly worked on the aircraft on the day, to the banks of Air Traffic Controllers sitting behind their scopes, both military and civilian alike, to ensure the deconfliction of the aircraft in the sky, to the obvious skill of those crews flying the aircraft, this is the story of how it all came together. From conception to planning, constant changes and contingencies, this flypast really was a 'once in a generation' event. Thanks to all those involved, it delivered the core message of the Royal Air Force at its Centenary birthday; the first Independent Air Force to achieve this milestone – it Commemorated those who went before us, it Celebrated the global work the Royal Air Force and its people do today and it undoubtedly served to Inspire the future generation.

*Chapter 2*

# Conception – Building the Flypast

## November 2016 – 2017

'What an amazing opportunity and privilege!' was my first thought as Group Captain (now Air Commodore) Steve Ward OBE asked in November 2016 whether I would consider taking on the role of planning and coordinating the flypast as part of the RAF 100 celebrations scheduled for July 2018. Being late 2016, I was just a couple of months into my role as the Chief of Staff of the Tornado GR4 Headquarters at RAF Marham and was busy getting to grips with the staff work side of working in this role.

The flypast was over eighteen months away but I immediately said yes and then rapidly wondered what on earth I had just agreed to. I knew it was going to be a once-in-a-lifetime experience, outstrip any previous event I had planned and would also undoubtedly occupy a large chunk of time. I wondered how I would actually fit it all in among the rest of the day-to-day work which goes on in an operational front-line Force Headquarters which has a significant proportion of its units abroad. As a Force, we would also be dealing with managing the drawdown and retirement of the aircraft fleet and moving on its personnel as the aircraft type was due to go out-of-service on 31 March 2019. Nothing like a good bit of prioritisation, and at this range, the key would be to start early and identify the long-lead items required to deliver the flypast. These would need to be tackled first. At this stage I knew very little about how flypasts such as these would be put together but I knew the concepts of planning and briefing large exercises involving multiple aircraft. I had both planned and led plenty through my career. Typically, these exercises involved large numbers of aircraft departing multiple airfields, holding prior to the 'push', deconflicting throughout the mission with the aim of striking various simulated targets at or within a specified time window. There was the added complication of 'enemy aircraft' and simulated surface-to-air missile systems trying to prevent us getting to the targets. Conceptually, however, the planning – whether an air exercise or a flypast – would be very similar in that we had to dispatch and recover a large number of aircraft from airfields while putting them over a piece of sky at a particular time. The similarities were therefore striking when planning for a flypast, although we hoped for no enemy interaction! Thankfully, for the differences, there would be the ability to learn about building London flypasts as we had also been given the task of putting together the Queen's Birthday Flypast in June 2017, so contacts, key stakeholders and procedures would be learnt first before tackling the big one. Not that we could afford a Birthday Flypast to be anything other than a success mind you, Her

Majesty the Queen, the public and TV cameras would very much be watching. Our headquarters would also be given the Queen's Birthday Flypast in June 2018 to manage as well. While this sounds like a lot, and it is, as with many of the type of events we do, we would not be starting from scratch. There was a wealth of information from previous years about the timescales, contacts and procedures for the delivery of Queen's Birthday Flypasts and I had acquired the files and paperwork to help with understanding all of these procedures and lessons. We also had the information from the Jubilee flypast from 2012 to hand. But regardless, this Centenary flypast would be different and I knew it. For a start it would be far larger – the number '100' was an obvious starting point, whether as a formation type or total number of aircraft. During November and December of 2016, the first sets of ideas about what would constitute the flypast were generated. Numbers of aircraft, formations, overall scale and an array of ideas were set in slides and pictures as to what would constitute the flypast. The key element of focus at the start was what would constitute the centrepiece. Understanding the scale was critical and all of the ideas we had would require large numbers of aircraft so a key decision which had to be addressed very early on was how much of an impact each Group could accept and still maintain the very necessary operational and training outputs (the RAF is divided into Groups, the relevant ones to the flypast being: No 1 Group consisting of combat and surveillance aircraft, No 2 Group being transport, cargo and air-refuelling aircraft, and No 22 Group consisting of training aircraft. Joint Helicopter Command would also be providing any helicopter assets required). Within each Group sits the individual squadrons. We needed to understand and factor in operational deployments, overseas and UK exercises as well as any other pertinent obligations that would prevent or limit participation in the flypast. The initial trawl went out to all of the Groups asking for participation options and numbers. We obviously had one hundred aircraft in mind right from the start, although the Chief of the Air Staff, Air Chief Marshal Sir Stephen Hillier, was keen to emphasise that this was not to be met at all costs – regard for our personnel, other operational activity and, of course, safety would be paramount. I was confident it could be done though, but it would require nearly every flying unit that the RAF had to be able to put that many aircraft airborne on the day, but even then, there was no guarantee that we would have our full complement. The challenge of understanding what was available to us became all the more difficult as operational requirements would dictate what was available rather than the other way around. The draw on each squadron can change in an instant depending on world events. As such, we needed to factor this flexibility in the planning from the start, keenly aware that it would be constantly changing, maybe even up to the day prior to the flypast.

## Theme of the flypast

With the celebration of one hundred years of the Royal Air Force, one element we discussed early on in the planning phase was how we may be able to theme the flypast.

One option was to see whether we could run formations through, starting with the oldest aircraft to the newest. Would it therefore be possible to date-order the flypast which would necessitate the Battle of Britain Memorial Flight with their DC-3, Hurricanes, Spitfires and Lancaster being first, and then end it with the finale being the brand-new F-35 Lightning aircraft – aircraft which were still not in the country at this point. In between the DC-3 and F-35 would be a mix of aircraft formations as they aged through the intervening years. In principle the general idea was sound, fitted within the one-hundred-year theme nicely, and allowed the RAF to showcase its full range of aircraft and capabilities. We wanted full representation where possible from every aircraft type.

We spent some time engaging with the Groups on what they could provide for the flypast, noting the challenge of the unknown events in the eighteen or so months ahead. We got to a position where each Group had tentatively agreed on numbers of participants. From there we could start formulating potential formation options in terms of what they would look like in the sky. Breaking down discrete aircraft types into formations gave us an initial one hundred and one aircraft split into fifteen separate formations, with the option of adding in the new Juno and Jupiter training helicopters if needed. At this stage, although we asked, the option of using the new Phenom, Texan and Prefect training aircraft was not available to us. The delivery of the new UK Military Flying Training System (MFTS) into which these aircraft fitted was still transitioning through its early stages and contractually there may have been some issues with providing the level of support we would require. The overall idea of using MFTS aircraft was parked at this stage but remained as a possible option as the months ticked by. To have them present would again have fitted in well with demonstrating the new aircraft that the RAF would be acquiring.

Having said that the theme we wished to present would be a running order of old to new, we were immediately presented with a number of issues with this idea: the most challenging to overcome being the speed differences of each aircraft type which would participate in the flypast. Having spent some time working through the in-to-service date of each aircraft (as well as other methods of deciding who should lead whom, as it wasn't simple – was it the in-to-service date in the RAF, aircraft manufacture date etc), the layout on a page showed a complete mix of the aircraft types across the whole flypast with slow formations intermingled with the faster ones. This was highly problematic.

Following the old-to-new theme, our oldest and therefore lead aircraft was the DC-3. Its optimum cruising speed was 120 knots. It wouldn't want to fly much slower. Following the DC-3 would be the remainder of the Memorial Flight consisting of the Lancaster, Spitfires and Hurricanes which would fly at 165 knots. The DC-3 could not go that fast and as part of the safety case for operating single-engine aircraft over Central London, the fighter aircraft, in formation with the

Lancaster, could not go below 150 knots – operating above this minimum would give the fighters a much better ability, should the unthinkable happen and their engine fail, to be able to glide clear and ditch in the Thames or find open ground to land. We had to have two separate formations. All of the aircraft from the Battle of Britain Memorial Flight would be very limited in the speed range at which they could fly, and we also needed to cater for a headwind or tailwind on the day to allow aircraft to speed up or slow down to make their exact time over the Palace. The DC-3 at 120 knots and Lancaster/Fighter formation at 165 knots were near fixed on speed. The challenges emerged when looking at the third formation. Despite not strictly following the old-to-new theme, we knew it had to be a helicopter formation next due to their slower but similar speeds. All subsequent aircraft following the third formation would be flying at least double their speed so the helicopters would have to go in front of them. They were normally the slowest participants and typically cruised along at 90 knots, or about 105 mph. Their position in between a formation flying at 165 knots and the formation behind which would be at 180 knots meant that there would be a sequencing and overtake issue as they approached the Palace. We would have to deal with the sequencing and overtake issue, but I was confident that this would be resolved with some careful planning, such as manipulating their final routing as they approached the Palace, as well as possibly amending some of the timings between the formations. The same issues reoccurred as we date-ordered the flypast, although we had some extra flexibility in selecting aircraft speeds as the aircraft got faster. It was problematic, but at the earliest stages it seemed we could overcome the issue.

Concurrent in thought was the production of the centre-piece of the flypast. Designing and then delivering it was always going to be ambitious and we looked to previous years' formation flypasts to give an understanding of what the art of the possible would be. Many of the large formations that we reviewed were extensions of standard large formations, such as the diamond 16 of Harrier jets flown in 2010. An 'EIIR' formation had been flown by Jet Provosts in 1968, as well as more recently by Hawks in 2012 for the Queen's Diamond Jubilee. A '60' formation had also been part of the same event, so this is what we looked at in more detail. The possibility of scribing either 'RAF' or '100' in the sky would, at least on paper, be achievable. Both formations, however, would require large amounts of aircraft – the 'EIIR' had required twenty-seven aircraft and the '60' used twenty. Lesser options as a centre-piece were also needed and at the most basic we had options ranging from multiple formations of nine aircraft forming diamond patterns from the various fleets participating, through to the more ambitious sixteen aircraft formation which the Harrier Force had flown at its retirement. While not usual, the diamond 9 formations are still flown, albeit infrequently, and, as multiple formations would fly them, it would not have been a true centre-piece for the Centenary. The sixteen-ship option was better, but it just didn't feel that this formation either would be justifiable given the grandness of the event. The two most obvious but ambitious options were to scribe either the 'RAF' or '100' formations in the sky.

Having drawn the aircraft layout on paper, we knew that forming an 'RAF' in formation would require twenty-nine aircraft. We also knew that the only flying unit which would have enough aircraft to even come close to filling this requirement would be the Typhoon Force. We would need eleven aircraft to form the 'R', ten to form the 'A' and eight to form the 'F'. Interestingly, the experiences gleaned from talking to the Hawk pilots who flew the 'EIIR' formation in 2012 gave us valuable insights as to the difficulties with flying this particular formation. For the 'RAF' formation, there were challenges with assuring aircraft safe separation which went hand-in-hand with a lack of suitable references, particularly in the 'A' for pilots to fly against. References are critical to safe and accurate formation flying. Pilots use them to maintain a steady position on the other aircraft, normally by means of lining up various features while looking at the aircraft and then keeping them stable. It may be a wing tip light which has to line up with a particular aerial, or ensuring that the engine exhausts remain squared off. Whatever it is that is used, it allows every pilot to fly and maintain the same formation position. There are normally at least two separate references, if not more, that need to be kept in check. It is this constant monitoring and position amendment which makes the work tiring. Both the throttle and stick are moving almost constantly. If you then throw in a bumpy day, as air is rarely completely still, it makes it even more challenging. Flying in formation is a skill practised from the earliest days of flying training, but the references selected are only against one other aircraft. In some of the positions the pilots would fly in the 'RAF' formation, the accuracy of being in the right place meant that multiple references across more than one other aircraft would be required. This may mean the pilot having to switch their viewpoint constantly between other aircraft. While achievable, this is very challenging and the likelihood of poor position-keeping would be high. The ripple effect, as aircraft continually jostle to maintain position, across the rest of the formation could be dangerous as movement can become amplified down a line of aircraft in formation. With amplified movement, pilots may well need to action an emergency break-out to avoid a collision. Having these break-out options should the pilot need to quickly get out of the formation is standard practice but in much larger formations such as the ones we were planning, sometimes the only break-out options would be either up or down. There was simply no room to sharply turn the aircraft left or right or decelerate. If the references were poor, it would make it very difficult to maintain the required positions and for the ground observer it would mean that the formation would look sloppy, the aircraft out of position and at its worst make the letters appear un-formed. Notwithstanding the safety aspects, this whole situation was something we had to avoid. I am in no doubt that the 'RAF' formation could have been managed with significant practice but even as it was being discussed, most preferred the option of flying a '100' down the Mall. It fitted far more with the Centenary theme and would look just as incredible, if not more.

There were various options in how we would form the '100' as the centre-piece. The first decision to be made was about the overall size of each of the individual elements. We had seen with the 2012 Jubilee '60' that the '0' had been formed with ten aircraft. So, we based the initial picture on that and saw that we needed twenty-six aircraft. This would place ten in each of the '0's and six (or five, depending if we wanted the '1' to look like a straight line) for the '1'. It would be smaller, but not by much, than the previous 'RAF' formation. Going for twenty-six aircraft at this stage was ambitious but also gave us flexibility – we could reduce the whole formation by five aircraft if required. The '0' could be formed by eight aircraft and the '1' by just five and it would still retain the symmetry. Whichever option was eventually selected, the pilots we spoke to were confident that this was a far friendlier formation to fly as the positions would be more akin to the positions normally flown. The most challenging position would be the final aircraft in each of the '0'. They would still have to reference off up to three aircraft to maintain their symmetry – the aircraft left and right of them as well as the aircraft leading at the front of the '0'. It still wouldn't be easy.

Content that we would want to fly a '100', the next thing to decide was how we were going to display it. The first option was to fly each individual element in line astern, i.e. the '1' would lead the '0' which would lead the second '0'. There was, of course, a sub-set to this as well. The elements could be flown two ways as shown:

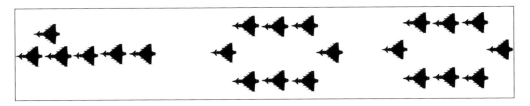

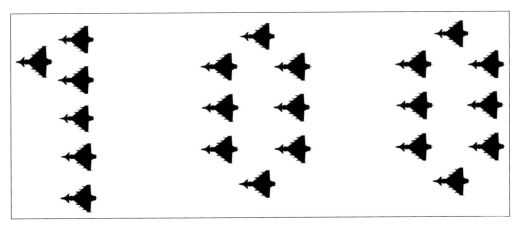

These options provided some significant benefits in that it was easier to fly – certainly the first one. In both options, the three elements were more individually manoeuvrable on the run-in. The narrow width of the formation also meant that we could be assured that the public watching from the length of the Mall, with the trees either side, would definitely see it. The first option also lent itself nicely to the critical break-out options as previously discussed and flying mostly in a line-astern position was far easier in maintaining reference position and therefore looking well-formed from the ground. These options were both viable and were put in the mix for selection.

The third option was to approach and fly down the Mall with the whole thing set as a lateral formation with all three elements next to each other from left to right. The profile would seem backwards when flown from the vantage point of the cockpit as the '1' would be on the right-hand side, with the two '0's to the left of it. This, of course, meant that from the ground an observer would see the formation pictured correctly. However, putting this formation together laterally meant it would be more challenging to fly. It would have to be flown as one whole unit rather than three as

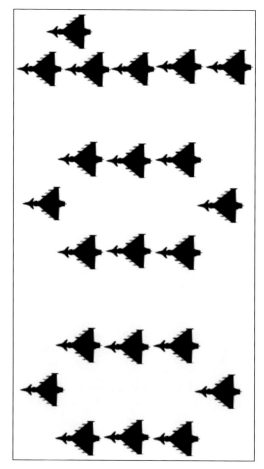

the previous options. Although the layout was designed such that obtaining and maintaining the references which the pilots would need would be simpler than the 'RAF' formation, it was still a lot of aircraft in one particular part of the sky. Break-out procedures would have to be carefully thought through. Manoeuvring the formation into position so it was lined up perfectly down the Mall would also be far more difficult. It would be like trying to turn an oil tanker – perfectly possible but slow and steady. Movement of the formation meant each of the three main elements which formed the '100' would need to move at the same time. If they didn't there would be a very real risk of collision. We also had concerns regarding the width of the formation – would the crowd be able to see it all? We suspected that it would be fine, noting the height they would be flying at, but we wanted to be sure. Further analysis of this would have to come once we definitely knew which aircraft would participate and could then start working out the actual dimensions of the completed formation. Thus, the final option that was considered is shown pictorially on the previous page.

In the illustrations thus far, only the silhouette of the Typhoon is shown but this was not always the case. True, with the weight of numbers required, there was only one Force who could fly either the 'RAF' or '100' in toto and that was the Typhoon Force. However, the initial ideas looked at various options of having all three elements of the '100' being flown by different aircraft. For example, the Tornado GR4 could form the '1', with the Hawks and Typhoons forming the respective '0's. We experimented with various ideas and put all of these various formations on some PowerPoint slides and tried to envisage what they would look like in the air, and more importantly from the ground. A couple of issues immediately came to the fore. First, the difference in size between the Hawk and the other fast jet aircraft may have caused the '100' to look unbalanced or 'skinny' in one area. Second, there would be far more coordination and practice sorties required due to the dissimilar aircraft contained in the formation. There are specific rules regarding dissimilar aircraft in formation and although far from insurmountable, it would create an additional training burden on the three different fleets of aircraft. Spare capacity is not something that is ever in great supply and two out of the three fleets had continuous and demanding front-line operational roles. The Hawk fleets, of which we had two from which to choose, were no simpler. The Hawk T2 aircraft from IV Squadron at RAF Valley were busy providing critical training for pilots going through the flying training system. If we chose the Hawk T1s from 100 Squadron at RAF Leeming, there would be a reduction in the provision of aggressor and close air support training for the Army and RAF as we got closer to the event. Although we planned to use these squadrons within the whole flypast, possibly as smaller stand-alone formations, the practice requirements for the '100' would be far greater. Notwithstanding all of this, it was deemed that we would most likely be able to share the burden across three fleets rather than one and therefore, because we had split the load, the likelihood of the successful delivery of the centre-piece was higher. However, as scoping continued, the capacity limitations became ever more evident. With much of the Tornado fleet deployed abroad it was highly unlikely that we would get the ten aircraft available and airborne to form a '0' and then have capacity for providing additional spare aircraft to cater for any airborne unserviceabilities. Even reducing the requirement to eight to form the '0' helped little – the Force may well be too stretched and we did not have the confidence to proceed. Additionally, the Hawks were deemed somewhat too small to match the size of the other jets and even on paper it just didn't look quite right. The one Force we did have confidence with was the Typhoon Force. They were incredibly busy and would still need to hold their UK Quick Reaction Alert throughout but they were the largest Force by far. After balancing these factors and likely availability, a hybrid option was deemed best and this would consist of six Tornado GR4s which would form the '1', and twenty Typhoons forming the '00'.

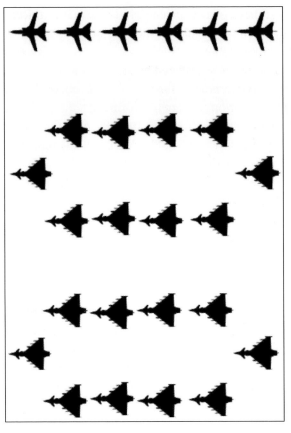

A number of discussions continued to be had over the presentation of the '100' which ultimately led to the selection of the lateral '100' – the third option as depicted above. It would certainly be harder to fly but despite the more challenging aspects associated with flying this formation, we deemed that the visual aspect from the ground would be far more impressive and the consensus among the crews who would be flying it was that it would be achievable. We had our centre-piece.

Early on in this conception phase, consideration was given to the possibility of whether, and to what extent, we should seek to incorporate the other Services' aircraft, other international air forces' aircraft, as well as any pertinent ex-RAF but civilian-owned aircraft. The obvious Service links were the amalgamation of the Royal Naval Air Service and the Army's Royal Flying Corps to form the Royal Air Force in April 1918, as well as paying tribute to the close collaboration of the three Services ever since – even if they didn't always see eye-to-eye! We would already have helicopters operating under the Joint Helicopter Command so a link with the Army was already established. The Joint Helicopter Command would be providing the Puma and Chinook aircraft. The expectation of using the F-35 Lightning – a joint asset between the Royal Navy and the RAF was there, but we also considered the use of the Royal Navy Historic Flight (RNHF). Similar in set-up to the RAF's Battle of Britain Memorial Flight, the RNHF had on its books a Chipmunk, Sea Fury, Sea Hawk and two Swordfish aircraft. Of these aircraft, only the Chipmunk had actually seen service with the RAF in the 1960s. The Swordfish aircraft in the Flight had not been in actual RAF service, although the RAF flew the type in the late 1930s and into the Second World War. The plan for the flypast was understandably quite light on historic aircraft and these would have made great additions and would have fitted nicely in the initial flypast concept proposed of date-ordering aircraft from old to new. Both aircraft would be flying very slowly and would have been positioned in the front-end of the flypast. The Swordfish would have gone ahead of the DC-3. The concern here was that the opening impact would, in many respects, have been quite muted. Being the slowest of the formations the Swordfish aircraft would lead, but being so few of them it would have looked somewhat lack-lustre. The same could be said of incorporating the Chipmunk (and for the same reason, it was decided that the BBMF Chipmunk was not to be used). Despite being a type that the RAF flew in the 1930s and '40s, the Swordfish was predominately a Naval aircraft. That fact, combined with it being a single-engine aircraft (there are risks we needed to consider – more later), and being flown by the Royal Navy on what was the RAFs Centenary celebration took it out of the running. Having either of the other two Services leading the RAF's flypast would have been somewhat an odd message to send to the nation!

It was not just the BBMF or RNHF which operated aircraft from bygone RAF eras. Internationally, the option of incorporating 'Vera', the only other airworthy Lancaster, was considered. It would have made a fantastic spectacle as both the BBMF Lancaster and 'Vera' flew in formation down the Mall. But, unfortunately, due to a variety of factors this couldn't be taken forward. There were a large number of civilian operators as well. We tentatively thought about approaching the array of civil operators that had aircraft still operating in the UK which could be used as part of the flypast. BAE Systems approached us early on and offered us the use of their Avro Anson Mk19. The twin-engine Anson had a very long and distinguished service history with the Royal Air Force and would have made a very interesting addition. Currently sporting a bright blue colour scheme, the type entered service in March 1936 and remained so until 1968. Versatile and capable as a platform, the aircraft would have added more to the historic nature of the flypast. Ultimately, using this aircraft, along with the idea of asking further civilian operators to participate, came down to risk appetite, training requirements and reputational damage should an accident or incident occur. There may well have been additional commercial costs to factor in. The final option considered was incorporating other air forces' aircraft. It was problematic in that given the highly international character of the RAF, especially during the Second World War, it would be difficult deciding who would be asked to participate and with what aircraft. In the end the Chief of the Air Staff decided it would remain a purely UK line-up. This certainly decreased complexity and removed the challenges of fully risk-managing an international flypast over central London. While the overall safety of all of the aircraft was of no concern, the addition of international as well as civilian aircraft would have increased the overall level of risk and we would have had limited control over these assets. We needed the smallest amount of risk as possible so again, it was decided early on that these options would not be taken further. A large number of the older aircraft types operated were also single-engine aircraft. These carried their own unique risks. We already had a large number of single-engine aircraft operating within the flypast and this needed additional consideration.

Single-engine aircraft over London are a problem. At first glance it doesn't seem too much to be concerned about, but at the heights the formation would be flying, there was little in the way of options should the worst happen and their sole engine fail. The route, once it entered London airspace, was rather limited in terms of glide-clear areas; we had the River Thames and tentatively there were the London parks, although frankly these would most likely be full of people enjoying their lunch in the midday sun. There were also lots of trees. As such, they would not make great crash-landing areas. Although an unusual and rare event, engine failures are a very real risk and therefore single-engine aircraft required due consideration as to their participation in the flypast. While it wouldn't necessarily stop the use of these aircraft, the risk needed to be balanced and justified against the perceived reward. Conceptually, we needed the single-engine aircraft. It wasn't just about making up the numbers. The Red Arrows, for starters, had to be present and each of the other single-engine aircraft, the Tucano, Hawk and F-35 Lightning demonstrated a different aspect of the Royal Air Force of today. We wanted to showcase each. Other than just plain good airmanship and safety, we had to satisfy rules regarding glide-clear options should the engine fail. These are set down in both the civilian Air Navigation Order as well as replicated in our own Military Aviation Authority regulations. In short, aircraft should not fly over built-up areas lower than that height which would enable them to glide clear should their engine fail. At 1,000ft, we would be beneath this height and thus in contravention of the regulation. We needed to apply for a waiver, but to do that we had to go into mathematical detail to assess how long the risk lasts and match that against the probability of the failure of the engine. Each year we always generate single-engine safety cases for the Red Arrows and the Battle of Britain Memorial Flight fighters to participate in the Queen's Birthday Flypast, so in essence this would be no different. Except it would be bigger. We normally would only have up to, say, eleven aircraft to assess, but for this flypast it was in excess of forty. Not only did we need to assess the individual risk for each aircraft but we then needed to consider the cumulative effect of all of the participants in the flypast. Only if the overall risk was negligible would we continue. It was also evident that the overall risk would need to be held at the highest level – while assessed as a very remote possibility, the damage could be huge and would have significant societal impact. We were mindful of this as well as all the other contingencies we had to plan for throughout. Over a period of months, and once we had collated all of the safety cases and assessed them, we sought a waiver through the Military Aviation Authority which was duly granted. Single-engine failure, through whatever cause, was the main issue that concerned us as a team throughout. Ultimately, as the Senior Duty Holder, the Chief of the Air Staff weighed all the advice and decisions and signed off against the overall flypast risk.

At the opposite end of the spectrum was the inclusion of the largest and heaviest aircraft in the RAF's inventory. Number 2 Group, home to all transport, air refuelling and cargo aircraft, and Number 1 Group, home to our large surveillance and reconnaissance aircraft were approached to see what could be available for the flypast. A collection of these aircraft, flying at 1,000ft, would look incredibly impressive and also demonstrate some of the capabilities of the RAF. Ever in short supply and often operated as very small fleets, it was always going to prove a challenge to get them in any great numbers. Still, we were optimistic and sought to showcase a large number of these aircraft. We also wanted an impressive showpiece. There were options about putting the fast-jet aircraft adjacent to the large aircraft in an echelon formation, as well as simply having the large aircraft by themselves. We seemed to have many options. We knew that some of the aircraft fleets would simply not have the numbers to commit to anything more than one aircraft – namely the E-3D Sentry or the Rivet Joint. These, however, would look impressive regardless. What is rarely seen is a close formation of large aircraft and it was here that we sought to generate a further spectacle. It came in the form of putting four C-130 Hercules in one formation followed by four Atlas in a formation. Such large aircraft so close would look incredible. We gained agreement in principle but were always conscious that we may be over-extending ourselves in optimism. We hoped that there would be enough airframes available.

From starting in November 2016 to the first draft of a flypast by March 2017, we had a basic plan. These collections of ideas were presented to the RAF's hierarchy and was partially agreed in principle. Traditionally the Red Arrows had always concluded the large flypasts for a number of good reasons. Other than the nine red Hawks naturally seeming like a fitting conclusion for a flypast, the smoke left in their wake could potentially cause visibility problems for aircraft following. Despite this, I wanted to change this round to follow the old-to-new theme where possible and have the Reds at a different position in the overall formation. I knew that it would look very odd placing them in the middle of the formation, which is where their 'age' would place them, so they ended up being just ahead of the F-35s, with an option of the F-35s being nestled in the Red Arrows formation, similar to what the Reds had done with Concorde some years earlier. It was not to be so. The main change following the discussions at this stage was that the Red Arrows were to be the finale piece and set behind the F-35s. The options of using other Naval or civilian aircraft were also formally closed. But what we did have was clear direction and a semblance of a running order.

The initial flypast concepts and basic mission planning had considered all aspects that we would feasibly know about at the time. Things would continue to evolve as we moved from the concept phase into actual planning. One element that was stark, even at this basic level was that there was no way we could feasibly manage the timing and speed issues to deliver a true old-to-new concept. These issues were proving impossible to resolve as the next chapter will illustrate. As part of the concept phase, the bones of the entire formation had been built – it was nowhere near complete, but bridged the concept into the planning phase with sufficient detail that would remain. The formation as it stood – now labelled with an overall Air Traffic Control callsign of '*Windsor Formation*' – looked as follows:

| | |
|---|---|
| First formation | DC–3 |
| Second formation | Lancaster with 4 Spitfires and 2 Hurricanes |
| Third formation | 3 Pumas followed by 10 Chinooks |
| Fourth formation | 9 Tucanos |
| Fifth formation | 2 King Airs |
| Sixth formation | 4 Hercules |
| Seventh formation | 4 Atlas |
| Eighth formation | 1 Sentinel and 2 BAe 146 |
| Ninth formation | 1 Voyager and 2 C17 |
| Tenth formation | 1 Rivet Joint |
| Eleventh formation | 1 Sentry |
| Twelfth formation | 6 Hawk T1 |
| Thirteenth formation | 9 Hawk T2 |
| Fourteenth formation | '100' consisting of 6 Tornado GR4 as the '1' and 20 Typhoons making up the two zeros |
| Fifteenth formation | 3 F–35 Lightning leading the 9 Red Arrows |

We had one hundred and one aircraft due to take part, plus spare capacity allocated. As we will see, this initial plan changed somewhat as the planning process progressed but it was enough to allow the real commencement of the intricate planning process which would last until July 2018. As the year progressed, there were also inklings that we were to put on an additional flypast over the Royal International Air Tattoo at Fairford, just three days after the London event. This would mean building a completely new plan and come with significant additional workload. Right now, I quietly hoped that it just remained an inkling.

## Chapter 3

# Making it a Reality

We had a general conception of what the flypast would now look like, but this, despite taking some months to gain agreement, was really just the beginning. Although we had agreements about who would be participating, a rough concept of formations and the overall size and scale, we now needed to start the challenging task of building the flypast plan which the aircrew would fly. This was a complex task and it was much like a gigantic jigsaw puzzle where each piece placed would directly affect the other parts and allow further progression. It would also affect the wider air community including civilian airspace users and have a significant impact on the workload in Air Traffic Control.

One of the very first actions was to start trying to fathom out in broad but accurate terms how much airspace the flypast would need to fly through. Overflight of Buckingham Palace by a flypast always impacts the operations at London Heathrow airport and this one would be no different. Flypasts such as these require large volumes of sanitised airspace to maintain safety – not just for the aircraft participating but also for all other air users. No one wants an Air Prox (where aircraft get too close) or worse, a collision with another airspace user. This can be mitigated on the whole by surrounding the flypast by a block of airspace known as a RA(T) or Restricted Airspace (Temporary). This is a three-dimensional block of segregated airspace into which only specified users are allowed. We knew it would cover a large geographical area but of course, we would not need it all to be active for the entire duration of the flypast, so we could divide it into areas. Each area can be time-bound so we would be able to specify which particular areas were active for which particular times. This would have the effect of minimising the impact to other flying operations, be that airliner activity out of Heathrow or light aircraft flying out of the myriad of small airfields in the south of England. As you can imagine, altering the pattern of flying in to and out of somewhere like Heathrow requires a massive degree of coordination and forward planning to minimise any delay. In order to start generating this and commence the engagement with the Civil Aviation Authority (CAA) to arrange and approve the airspace, we needed to have a very good idea of exactly how much airspace and time was required. Once the airspace requirements were set, there was very little that we would be able to do to amend them. It had to be right first time, or if it was wrong we would have to make our plan fit inside the airspace that we had deemed necessary at the beginning.

Hand-in-hand with the airspace requirement would be the generation of a skeleton plan complete with routes for each aircraft or formation to fly. As much as I would wish for simplicity, it is not as easy as just giving every aircraft a time to be over the Palace and then hoping that they would meet up in the right part of the sky, at the right time, with all other formations and make it work. For a variety of reasons, this plan would be doomed to failure. Problems with aircraft serviceability on the ground, delayed take-off clearances, weather reroutes once airborne or other air traffic could all conspire to almost guarantee failure if this method were used. There was also the minor issue of coordinating with many other aircraft within the formation as well as ensuring that their ingress and egress routes did not run them into confliction with each other. We also had to ensure that the air traffic controllers were not overwhelmed with sheer numbers. To manage this and set the flypast up for success, the overall plan was split into constituent parts and they all required large areas of airspace to safely achieve it. Experience from managing large airborne exercises meant that we knew we would build holding areas, ideally positioned over the sea. This would allow a degree of flexibility of time to hold as well as providing geographical space where crews could bring their formations together. From the holding areas, we would need routes to start funnelling the formations in towards Central London. Once the formations were perfectly aligned with the Mall and therefore the Palace, we would then need a sizeable portion of airspace to break apart the formations safely, ensuring that they were adequately deconflicted from each other so they could disperse and route back to their landing airfields.

Thankfully we had a basic blueprint. Each year in June, the Queen's Birthday Flypast typically uses a small holding-area over the sea off Southwold in the South-East of England. The exit from this hold aligns the aircraft with a straight run-in route which lines the aircraft up with the Palace. In the overshoot of the Palace a small dispersal area then allows aircraft to split apart and start the climb to height as they return back to their home bases. Even this standard block of airspace is large, but it would be nowhere near sufficient size. An average Queen's Birthday Flypast is often planned to be around thirty aircraft but this one was going to be over three times that size. Our airspace requirements were therefore somewhat bigger.

It was difficult to know exactly where to start. While the basic airspace blueprint and previous Queen's Birthday Flypasts gave us an understanding of what had worked before, the differences in scale gave us some additional problems. Logically though, starting with the first formation and planning each subsequent formation in turn seemed sensible. We also had to make some early educated assumptions about where aircraft would be based predominantly on their expected fuel range and time airborne. To help capture all of this on a plan, we had some excellent mission-planning software which would make the task of understanding the airspace requirements and building the plan somewhat easier. Technology was our friend here and our Mission

Planning Aid was capable of showing various types of aviation and scaled maps from 1:5,000,000 down to the familiar Ordnance Survey 1:50,000 maps along with high-resolution satellite imagery. We used it daily on the squadron to plan all of our missions, and so did the majority of the other flypast participants. Most importantly, it gave us the ability to overlay the routes of aircraft on to the maps, drag and drop the route as required, dictate their speed, turn radius and height as well as defining a host of other parameters which then allowed an output of accurate geographic and timing information. Once each route had been planned, it could be amended continually to ensure that the aircraft were planned to fly over the right piece of sky at the right time and also ensure we avoided areas where they weren't allowed to fly. The data generated from the mission software could then be loaded into the aircraft to give a route to fly as well as timing to follow. Crucially at this stage, it also allowed us to visually see how much airspace we would need.

We had barely started on building the draft plan when the first issue regarding the formation constitution emerged. The plan as shown in the previous chapter had the DC-3 first followed by the Battle of Britain Memorial Flight, thereby starting with the oldest aircraft and working up, thus demonstrating the old-to-new concept as best we could. It became evident that we would have to change. The 120 knot DC-3 was not the slowest aircraft in the flypast but it was in front of the remaining faster Second World War aircraft of the Lancaster, Spitfires and Hurricanes which were flying at 165 knots. Separated by time over the Palace, this wasn't the problem however. The problem was that both those formations were due to be ahead of the slowest participants, the Pumas and Chinooks which flew at a more leisurely 90 knots.

This had previously been identified as a problem that would need to be solved in our conception phase. So why was this such an issue?

It was fundamentally about the speed differential between the three formations combined with the fixed track that all of the aircraft would have to use to line up down the Mall. The DC-3, callsign *Dakota* would be travelling at 120 knots, *Memorial* at 165 knots and the helicopters at 90 knots. As standard, we had also used a fixed thirty second separation over the Palace between each formation. This separation allowed enough space between every formation for safety but not so much that there would be a big and noticeable gap for the public. We could have used a greater separation time but in truth it made little effect in resolving the issue. Due to the factors of a fixed final approach track to the Palace and timing constraints for consistency, the faster formations of *Dakota* and *Memorial* would need to overtake the helicopters on the run-in if they were to make their timings in the order of *Dakota*, *Memorial* and then the helicopters. Now this is manageable if the overtake is done at a distance with much higher speed differences, time separations, or if they were able to merge at distance and overtake with sufficient crossing angles. But with small speed differentials of just forty-five knots between *Dakota* and *Memorial*, who were just thirty seconds behind, and then the 90-knot helicopters being behind them, meant that this overtake would end up occurring very close to the Mall. The overtake manoeuvre would therefore probably be visible to the spectators down the Mall and if not them, then the highly zoomed TV cameras certainly would see it. This was not ideal.

With timing fixed, we racked our brains looking for solutions to achieve an overtake while seeking to mitigate the downsides associated with viewing and safety. To complete the overtake, we had options of over, under, around or with a high angle join. Over and under options were immediately ruled out. The lowest a formation could be was 1,000ft above the ground due to clearances from the buildings and our regulations, so going underneath was neither a safe or legal option. Going over the top would need a commensurately high cloud-base – something that was a risk to the flypast delivery overall anyway, so we didn't want to make it worse. The manoeuvre would also need a fine degree of coordination between the formations, clear and concise radio communications and would then need the high formation to descend in excess of 500ft to close onto their flypast height of 1,000ft. In the large formation that we had planned, this would look highly untidy and would prejudice success. The risks on this option far outweighed the positives and it would still look poor to the viewing public, again due to the close range at which it would all occur. The over option was scrapped as well.

The final two options hinged on either the *Dakota* and *Memorial* formations going around the slower helicopters, or joining ahead of the helicopters from a large crossing angle. These two looked the most promising. Again, for safety, *Dakota* and *Memorial* would need to overtake sufficiently wide of the helicopter formations, gain their station ahead on time before slotting into the fixed approach track to line them up down the Mall. This, once we plotted it all out on the mission-planning software, showed that it would still all occur just a few miles short of the Palace. Again, it was far from ideal and at that range it would look like a wall of aircraft coming towards the spectators with them only lining up at the last minute. Notwithstanding this issue, the lead pilots of the DC-3 and *Memorial* would also have to guarantee that they would be visual with the helicopters on the day, before they could safely complete their manoeuvre. If visibility was close to the limits, this could be a real challenge and provide significant additional workload in an already high-pressured environment. The issues were stacking up. Contingency planning also became more complicated – if they should be unable to gain and maintain visual contact, we would need to plan additional methods of escape to keep them clear. It would, therefore, also increase the likelihood of not having some of the most iconic historic aircraft from the RAF's history, present in the flypast. This would be unacceptable. The other option was a high joining angle from either the north or south. However, the same problems emerged and additionally the width of our Restricted Airspace channel into London would need to be increased to incorporate all of these changes. The cost/benefit analysis into these options were weighing heavily in the cost perspective.

We spent some time experimenting with differing approach angles, slight speed changes and different separation timings over the Palace to ensure all options had been explored, but there was no way of safely managing the negative aspects while maintaining the spectacle of the flypast. Whichever way it was planned, the overtake, which would look messy, would be seen by the public, have added additional risks into the plan and made contingency planning far more complex. Disappointingly, this whole idea of having the helicopters third in line had to be consigned to the bin.

The reworked schedule meant that the helicopters would now lead with the DC-3 and the historic Memorial Flight following behind. The speed for Memorial was also lowered to 150 knots. The changes to the front-end of the flypast proved that we needed to ensure that all subsequent formations were either co-speed, or faster than, the preceding formation to avoid the same problem occurring again later in the flypast train. We would have the heavy aircraft in the middle and fast jets at the end in speed order. Now that the reworked front end of the flypast was sorted, the rest of the formations would start to be built into the software to continue on our path of understanding the extent of airspace required. These changes were more fundamental, however, as it meant that the old-to-new theme would not be apparent. With this reality, combined with the Red Arrows now being the finale formation, the original concept of old-to-new had well and truly gone.

## The Big Holds

Now the front-end of the flypast was complete, the remaining formations were amended and I had continued the task of building each formation into our mission-planning software. Knowing the approach into London was fairly fixed, I concentrated on building where the aircraft would all hold prior to the event. A maximum of twenty individual aircraft or formations could be programmed into the software and I was using eighteen at this stage – all of the formations (separate F-35 and Red Arrows formations) plus an additional two for the '100'. This allowed us to split each element apart as managing twenty-six aircraft as a single entity would not have helped our deconfliction planning. Even though a single aircraft line on our software may have represented up to ten aircraft, it was sufficient at this stage to allow for the planning and generation of the whole airspace requirement. It was growing pretty large – even at this early stage, and it became increasingly obvious that very early engagement with the CAA would be required. Basing, and where aircraft would be coming from, played a critical part in understanding the complete airspace requirement. Following the resolution of the timing and deconfliction issue with the front-end of the flypast, another issue brought up a constraint. Fuel. The helicopters would be travelling from their bases at RAF Odiham and Benson and could not complete the full sortie without running short of fuel. Some aircraft had long-range fuel tanks fitted but this could not be relied upon for all in the formation. I needed to find a place for them to stop off prior to the flypast. Wherever we used had to be able to cater for housing at least fifteen helicopters, be able to administer appropriate amounts of fuel for them to take (or allowing RAF fuel bowsers on to site), not cost a small fortune in landing fees and be appropriately close to our route. I scoured the route looking for suitable places and came up with just a couple of possible options. After discussion with the helicopter crews, Stapleford was chosen as a good fit for all of our requirements. I can only imagine what they must have thought during my initial phone call, when I asked this small but busy airfield to house at least fifteen Chinook and Puma helicopters plus spare aircraft on their field for half a day some months in the future. Either way, they were very obliging and the first non-military base for use in the flypast was in place. It helped in that it was very close to the inbound route and thus the airspace we would need could remain unchanged. The helicopter crews visited the site and found it appropriate for their requirements. It would also act as their hold location as they could arrange their formation in the very close vicinity to the airfield. For the rest of the flypast formations however, it was not as simple.

For fixed-wing holding it was a different story and we had set a number of constraints to try to make it all the more manageable on the day to give us the best chance of success.

The desired outputs for planning the holding patterns were that:

- As many of the individual holds as possible should be over the sea so that we could minimise disruption to civilian airspace users over land
- Due to the ingress routing, the holds would need to be positioned off the coast near Southwold or just off the North Norfolk coast
- To use as few holds as possible
- To keep aircraft as low as possible (subject to a minimum height of 1,000ft)
- Each individual aircraft should be allocated an individual 'sanctuary' height which was also separated by 1,000 ft from all other aircraft
- To allow the safe exit of those aircraft so they could commence their run-in

Almost immediately some of these outputs became problematic. Lack of fuel reserves in some aircraft meant oversea holding was not going to be possible as the distance was too great. Due to the numbers and trying to keep aircraft heights as low as possible, combined with the 1,000-foot sanctuary requirement, meant we would need far more holds than originally desired. These holds were very much like those used at civilian airports. Aircraft would join them, fly in large circles or oblongs until their specific time came to depart. However, rather than keeping aircraft relatively high, we needed our aircraft as low as practically possible. Keeping the aircraft low was important for a number of reasons, and ultimately all to do with the end goal of being established at 1,000ft above ground level as the formation crossed the coastlines as they routed inbound towards London. At lower heights in the hold, formations would be more likely to be in sight of the surface and not therefore have to penetrate cloud – something that is rather problematic in a large formation and can take a significant amount of time to do safely. Timing, unsurprisingly, was a critical function. To ensure we had the lead formation over the Palace at 1300 hrs and each subsequent formation spaced by thirty seconds in trail, we would be asking every formation to ensure that they left the holding patterns within a timing tolerance of plus or minus five seconds and on their allocated flypast speed. Doing that while in a descent and possibly trying to negotiate clearing cloud cover is far trickier than already being established at a low height.

Following the switch in formation order, the DC-3 and remaining BBMF aircraft were the first fixed-wing aircraft for which we needed to look at holding patterns. They also had various other events to attend either side of the 10 July so their departure location was potentially variable. As an early assumption, it initially appeared that Southend would make a prime location to stage them out of. They had used the airfield before so it was a known entity. It would also ease the burden off Coningsby, their home base, which also had the large number of Typhoons to depart and recover later in the day. With the selection of Southend, it also meant an overland hold was far more appropriate. Holding overland also reduced their risk should their single-engine fighters have any problems, as a return to an airfield would be quicker. Their route was fairly simple and I placed a hold for all of those aircraft just to the north of Southend. The aircraft would have to hold in visual conditions so a low hold, around 1,000ft would be adequate. The hold would also be pretty much on track and only offset up-track by a few miles from where the helicopters would be so they would most likely be visual with them on the day.

The aircraft following the Memorial Flight was a formation of training aircraft – the Tucano. It had entered service in 1988 and had been a venerable workhorse training both pilots and navigators/weapons systems officers since. I had trained in the Tucano some years earlier when we flew from RAF Topcliffe in Yorkshire; the sole base now was close-by at Linton-On-Ouse. This again proved a problem with fuel and range, but there were a couple of choices. We either planned to fly them from Linton but land-away elsewhere to refuel, or start from a closer location which would then allow them to complete the flypast and then land back at Linton. I wanted to keep using military airfields as much as possible rather than civilian ones – we already planned on using Stapleford and Southend, but I didn't want to expand this. There were always additional costs involved in using civilian airfields and this needed to be kept to a minimum. Capacity at military airfields was at a premium in the south and east of England but we sought out options to forward-base them which would allow a landing back at Linton. This would draw the Tucano aircraft away from the busy southern airfields which would be part of the recovery of other aircraft. An option close to the inbound route was Wattisham. This was now an Army base but still had a usable runway. An old Lightning and then Phantom base in the 1960s and '70s, the airfield had still been used until relatively recently as a fast-jet diversion airfield. It wasn't able to be used for fast-jets anymore but an enquiry to their airfield manager showed that we could use it for helicopters and lighter aircraft. It seemed to fit the bill for our Tucano formation. On the day, they would get airborne, hold in the overhead of the airfield to form-up before heading inbound to London. The liaison with the airfield would continue, but using this airfield helped significantly with the planning process. The airfield was very close to the inbound routing and this again helped us to minimise the amount of additional airspace we would need.

It also made sense for the King Air aircraft to hold nearby as well. As there were only  two of them, I was less concerned as to where they would hold with regard to them being contained inside the Restricted Airspace. Despite departing from RAF Cranwell, they would have plenty of fuel and could be placed just north of the Tucano hold which would then allow them to join behind at the right time.

Next up came the start of the heavy aircraft. These would be far trickier. While they had more than enough fuel and range and could therefore hold anywhere, they came with other challenges. We had never had such a mass of large aircraft to manage before. With four Hercules, four Atlas, one Sentinel, two BAe 146, one Voyager, two C-17 Globemaster, one Rivet Joint and one Sentry, we had a lot to hold, join together as formations and then ensure they could join in the flypast train at the right place and right time. The current planned formations were impressive and looked as follows:

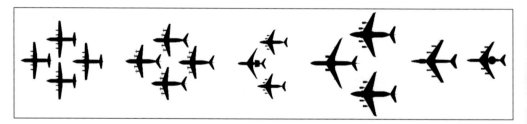

The key to success here would be to ensure that all the individual aircraft could enter their specific holds, join up as formations and then depart on time. I think that it is obvious, but I will make the point. Big aircraft don't generally do this very much – if at all. Both the pilots and air traffic control spend a great deal of time trying to keep large aircraft apart, not bring them together. When aircraft such as this enter a hold, it is normally to recover as a single entity to an airfield. While some of the aircraft types and crews had a degree of formation practice, there would need to be a good plan and a great deal of practice to ensure safety and success. In terms of the holding patterns and keeping the aircraft low, the minimum heights would still be 1,000ft. We also were not keen on mixing up formation types in holds where possible. It looked like we may need somewhere between five and six holding areas to make it happen. The original holding area at Southwold typically had only two or three previously. The area needed to be bigger and we still hadn't got to where we would hold the other fifty-three aircraft yet.

We had options of extending the holding area to the UK's Flight Information Regions (FIR) boundary. This was an imaginary line in the air which separated the airspace controlling authority between the UK and Europe. This gave an additional holding location bringing it to four. Four would be a compromise and manageable as the Hercules and Atlas formations would be given a hold each. The Sentinel and BAe 146s would have a separate hold and the Voyager / C17 formation would have the fourth. We reasoned that the Rivet Joint and E-3D would be able to join high in one of these holds and once the lower formations had all joined together, they could then lower themselves down through the stack and hold 1,000ft above them. In big picture terms, we were happy with this plan. Of course, it would need a lot of refinement but the airspace size could be made to work. They would all depart from and recover to their home bases of RAF Brize Norton and RAF Waddington, which made things simpler.

## The Fast Jet Formations

Similar to the Tucano fuel issue, we knew that there was going to be the same problem with both the Hawk formations. The first of the fast jet formations, the Hawk T1s, would be coming from 100 Squadron based out of RAF Leeming. Even without factoring in any holding time, they would not be able to make the full sortie if they departed and recovered to their home base. It was simply too far. The same could be said of the second Hawk formation which would be coming from IV Squadron based out of RAF Valley in North-West Wales. The initial plan, certainly for the 100 Squadron Hawks, was to use RAF Marham as their departure base. Being a current Tornado and shortly to be Lightning base, the airfield was perfectly suitable for Hawks and had, on the face of it, more than enough space for parking an additional nine aircraft. The services required by the Hawk would also be catered for – Marham had plenty of fuel and oils etc that would be needed for the aircraft after they landed. I spoke to Wing Commander Phil Marr, who ran the Operations side of the base, about the idea and we immediately hit a potential problem. The airfield was being prepared for the arrival of the F-35 Lightning and while there would be a runway available at all times through the period we would need it and the services required would be sufficient, it was not at all certain that there would be enough available parking and taxi space for all of the aircraft. We would, of course, also have the Tornado and Lightning aircraft operating from there as well. The airfield was going through a major infrastructure upgrade programme where some 90 per cent of the aircraft operating surfaces were, over a period of a couple of years, being dug up and relaid. On the various projections of what work would be done when, it appeared that right around the time of when we would want to utilise all of the hard-standing areas for parking, it would not actually be available. We debated this point over a few weeks as it was not entirely clear that the project timescales were indeed completely accurate. These things have a habit of not being on time – normally over-running, at which case we may well be alright. But needless to say, the sensible and least risky option became obvious. Finding an alternate plan later in the planning cycle would be challenging so we were left with finding another airfield for the Hawks to operate from.

Operating fast jets from non-home base options presents many additional considerations. Much of what can be considered as normal operating procedures can easily become much more challenging. Runway length, taxiways, parking spaces and fuel are the obvious concerns, but a variety of other aspects must also be considered. Engineering expertise and availability – the essential lifeline that supports all aircraft operations – is not as readily available once you depart the home base. Tools, test equipment and spares are no longer in-situ, and for the aircrew, access to mission planning, briefing areas and space to store their flying equipment may be

This perfectly highlights the amount of infrastructure work occurring at RAF Marham during the time of the flypast. With the uncertainty and lack of guarantee of exactly which operating surfaces would be available, we chose to not base further aircraft at RAF Marham. (© *Crown Copyright 2018, Cpl Jimmy Wise*)

non-existent or at a premium. It becomes even more challenging if much of the mission planning is done via software and those systems are located away at your home base. Of course, there are ways around all of this but it adds complexity and risk, the more austere the basing location. It is one of the reasons why aircrew conduct UK and foreign landaways during peacetime – to practice these skills for when they may truly be needed.

What we didn't need now was more risk, and the preference was still to try to use military bases where possible, certainly for the fast-jet operations. It was in discussion with Wing Commander Nick Badel, the Officer Commanding 100 Squadron, that the idea came up of using RAF Wittering as a land-away base. Halfway between Leeming and Marham, it would allow the Hawks to refuel the day prior, then complete their sortie and most probably be able to land back at Leeming post the flypast. RAF Wittering was an option I hadn't even considered. Now an elementary flying training base equipped with Grob Tutors, it used to be home to the Harrier Force before the aircraft type was withdrawn in December 2010 following the Strategic Defence and Security Review. As an ex-Harrier base, it certainly had a long enough runway. As there were flying units already operating from Wittering, many of the functions the Hawks would need, such as mission-planning areas and parking would be available. Wing Commander Nick Maxey was the Officer Commanding of the Operations Wing at Wittering and after a few phone calls and emails, Wittering became the take-off location for the 100 Squadron Hawks. It became a further deployed location to operate another formation from. Behind the scenes, this move also required the engineers to travel, taking along with them certain levels of spares, tools and other equipment to fix any minor problems with the aircraft should they arise.

Understanding where the Hawks would now be based allowed us to look at the detail as to how they would transit to a holding location. As with all of the other formations, the final ingress route was fixed, so we looked at where best to hold them.

The Southwold holding areas were now full with the heavy aircraft from the previous formations, so the Hawks were the first unit to be planned to use a new holding area off the North Norfolk coast. A hold for a fast-jet typically is around 8–10 miles in length. We wanted plenty of space for them so selected a nominal 30-degree bank angle for their turn at either end which, at the speeds they would be flying, gave a hold width of around 5 miles. In between each hold, we needed a suitable number of miles of separation to ensure that aircraft in each hold were adequately deconflicted from the other holds once they were established. With multiple holds required, this gave us a generally rectangular block of airspace that stretched from Cromer to the Wash and nearly as far north as Grimsby. It was all over the sea to minimise the impact to general civilian aviation but it would impact the helicopter operations that would need to transit out to the oil rigs in the North Sea. We would need to speak to the air traffic agencies who managed

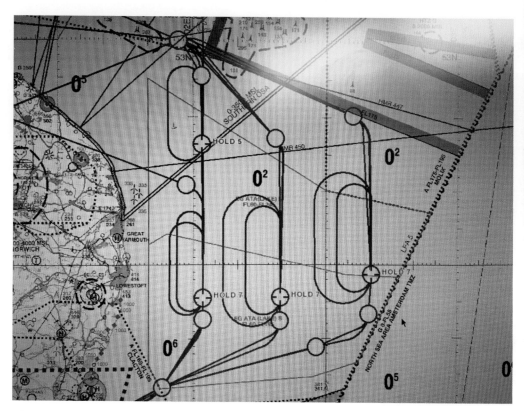

The Southwold Holds for the RAF 100 Flypast. Each line represents an individual formation. With our planning software, we were able to account for differences in speed, turn radius and aircraft track to show where each aircraft would fly. Aligned with timing, we could see exactly how each formation would leave the hold relative to other formations. (© *Crown Copyright 2018, Wg Cdr Kevin Gatland*)

this as well as Norwich airport who would be right in the middle of the planned Restricted Airspace to their north as well as to their east and south-east. We could probably get around four or five holds into this block of airspace and on a map, the combined holding areas looked large. I allocated the eastern-most hold to the 100 Squadron Hawks. Their route would nominally transit oversea before running down the eastern edge of the coastline before joining the main ingress route into Central London. The plan was already to use the North Norfolk holds for the centre-piece of the '100' and I wanted to keep the Hawk formations clear to give the '100' maximum space for their routing.

The second Hawk formation was based from RAF Valley, but again lack of fuel would preclude them from completing the full sortie from their home base. Once again, the search for appropriate airfields commenced. With options such as Marham and Coningsby already off the table, we had to look a little further afield. In the end, their selected option was Linton-On-Ouse. As the Tucanos vacated, the Hawk T2s would arrive. Linton was well known to all of the Hawk T2 pilots being a previous training base for them during their fast-jet training, so it'd almost be like a home from home. It did, however, create an issue in that they would not be able to recover back to RAF Valley due to the airborne time of the entire sortie. This wasn't ideal and we needed to plan for a landing location post-Buckingham Palace to allow them to stop off and refuel prior to getting back to RAF Valley. Despite being a helicopter base, RAF Odiham seemed a great choice and following their acceptance of the Hawks, the formation, now with the callsign *Ninja*, were allocated to recover there. Their holding area would be immediately adjacent to the 100 Squadron Hawks off the North Norfolk coast and I had again planned to route them down the eastern side of Norwich to follow thirty seconds in trail of them. Being so close in the holding pattern, they would almost certainly be visual with the other Hawk formation throughout the hold which would be beneficial when it came time to leave and route inbound towards London.

## Initial Planning of the '100' Centre-Piece

Being the key component to the entire flypast, the '100' formation needed to be as simple as we could possibly make it to give us the best chance of success. That really started from the take-off roll of each aircraft. Knowing that the aircraft would all depart in a stream, one after the other, the simplest plan would be to keep them low after take-off to minimise the chances of the formation being stacked very high through cloud. It would therefore also be far simpler if their holding areas could be as close to their departure bases of RAF Coningsby and RAF Marham as possible. This thinking drove the initial selection of the Wash and North Norfolk coast as their holding areas. The selection of these two locations also minimised the impact to the civilian sector by being oversea or contained within military danger areas.

For Tornado GR4 aircraft taking off from RAF Marham, it was an easy choice for their holding location. If they were held in the Wash danger areas known as the Holbeach range they would have a very simple route out, a short hold and could then join the correct side as the '1' of the formation. Their route would have them exit to the north east of the range and hook south-bound loosely joining the two '0's formed by the Typhoons to the east.

The initial Typhoon plan would see them depart RAF Coningsby and join up in the remaining two hold locations in the North Norfolk coast area. Their routing would be clear of all other aircraft formations entering the holds and seemingly was the simplest way to get the two sets of ten Typhoons together. They would be allocated individual sanctuary heights within these holds but hopefully would not need them as they could maintain visual or radar contact below any cloud. There were of course a number of contingency scenarios to be considered with this plan but at this early stage this plan worked.

Now it was onto the final two formations. It still wasn't certain that we would have the brand-new F-35 available to us but it needed to be planned in. Assuming that the aircraft had made their way over to the UK from the United States, it would take off from its home base at RAF Marham and due to the sensitivity of the new aircraft, it had to recover to RAF Marham as well. There were so many uncertainties at this stage as to what it could, or would, be able to do, including even knowing the performance of it at low level in terms of endurance and therefore range. We awaited the responses to our requests for information. Regardless, the plan again had to be simple and as short as possible. As it would be following the '100' formation, it made sense again for them to hold in the Wash along with the Tornado aircraft. As both the F-35s and Tornados would be coming from the same base, we reasoned that they could follow the Tornados out, establish in the same holding area before departing the hold at a thirty-second spacing to take up their position. All of the fast-jets would be travelling at a co-speed of 300 knots. The Red Arrows would then join from a separate route thirty seconds behind them.

The plan that was required for the Red Arrows was far simpler. They would need no hold to join as they would tag onto the back of the flypast train after following a route which allowed them to make good their timing. They also needed no real deconfliction or particular airspace consideration at this time. Their initial route would see them navigate to the east of RAF Coningsby, just over the sea before joining aboard.

At this stage we had a very good idea of where each formation would be taking off from as well as which hold they would be allocated to. The next stage was to apply a very basic routing to all of them which joined up their departure airfield to their hold, an exit from the hold and then fly as efficiently a route as possible to join the long run in track which lined up with the Mall and Buckingham Palace. Following an extended straight line from the Palace and Mall, the towns of Chelmsford, Colchester and Ipswich were almost in a direct line and would be able to witness the flypast procession as it flew overhead. Indeed, Ipswich was where the majority of the formations were planned to be meshing together to form the long train of aircraft. To align the aircraft properly in the right position in the formation, they also needed a time. So, a timing reference point was placed against each formation which allocated the time that they needed to be over the Palace. For the first helicopter formation, this was set at 1200Z or 1300 hrs local time. Each subsequent formation was given a thirty-second spacing which finished with the F-35s and then the Red Arrows at 1207:00Z. The crews needed to fly to this time on their allocated speed within plus or minus five seconds. As each of the aircraft were now in speed order, slowest to fastest, this naturally gave us an expected time that they would need to leave the hold. As a basic plan we now had the aircraft over the Palace in a deconflicted line. Much more work was required to finesse it but for the required purpose of airspace generation at this stage, so far so good.

## Egress – the Real Challenge

We had dealt with the airfield departure, hold entry, hold exit and basic route to the Palace but the real challenge of the plan was yet to come. The egress phase was the most critical, yet the vast majority of people watching would never know how much effort would go into this particular segment. As all of the aircraft closed in on the Palace they would also be catching each other up due to the increased speed of the formation behind. It was like a huge concertina. At the point of passing overhead the Palace, the individual formations would also be the closest they had been during the whole sortie. With all aircraft having made it to the Palace, we now had to plan the complete reverse of what we had done and try to split them all apart. At this initial stage in the planning cycle, all I really wanted to understand was the volume of airspace that it would take to enable this to occur safely. But as I started to get to grips with this, the requirement to understand the airspace volume meant planning out almost every formation in some level of detail to understand what would be required. To further complicate matters, the terrain also rises in the 30-40 miles in the overshoot of the Palace so aircraft would need to gently climb to maintain their minimum height above the ground. This would create an issue if the weather was fine over London but poor as the aircraft travelled further west. While we had weather limits for the flypast, we also needed to factor in the weather in the egress routes to ensure that it remained safe. This was especially important as it would take some time and distance to safely break apart the formations. The routes chosen needed, where possible, to remain in as low a ground as possible, which of course further complicated the deconfliction plan. This was important as a cancellation due to weather after the Palace rather than what everyone could see in Central London would be rather disappointing. We wouldn't be able to avoid all of the higher ground but we could try to mitigate it by thoughtful routing as best we could.

Getting the slow-moving helicopters and Battle of Britain Memorial Flight safely out of the way was the first concern. Individual aircraft are easy to manoeuvre, but formations – especially ones that are in close formation – are trickier. They would need to maintain their accurate positions because even after the Palace, the public would still be able to see them as they egressed away. We ideally wanted to avoid any dramatic manoeuvres where possible. But to clear the way from the rapidly closing faster formations, the helicopters had to route either hard to the left or right. Hard left was chosen, as the initial plan was to route them into Biggin Hill. This had a number of advantages, primarily in that it would keep them clear of all of the other aircraft egressing but also as it was a short route for fuel. It was a simple solution. The DC-3, Lancaster and Second World War fighters would follow a similar route to the south, with the DC-3 extending slightly further to the west before returning back to Southend. Again, this simple plan kept them nicely clear of all of the other egressing aircraft which would start to use new egress lanes to the west and north.

With London Gatwick to the South, we also ensured that their routes would not impinge on them. With impact to both Heathrow and London City, a third was far from desirable!

The egress options left available to us were to route aircraft north, between the Luton / Stansted airport gap or out to the west and north west. The northerly egress routes lent themselves nicely to the Tucano and King Air formations as they would have to route back towards Linton-on-Ouse and Cranwell. Both of these formations could come hard right, which deconflicted them well with the aircraft in front which had turned left, and also provided a heading directly towards their recovery bases. They would also be travelling at similar speeds so could almost follow each other north. We would have to think further about splitting up the 9-ship Tucano formation into smaller units but the plan worked at this stage as there was plenty of airspace for this to happen in. The formation could also split once it was north of the Luton/Stansted gap as the airspace was far more permissive. We also did not think that it would require additional Restricted Airspace as there would only be a relatively small amount of aircraft which would also start splitting up into smaller elements. This also kept the airspace requirement to a minimum.

For the Hercules, Atlas, Sentinel, BAe 146, Voyager, C-17, Rivet Joint and Sentry, we reasoned that they could all route out west, start a climb and either enter a holding pattern if required to recover to Brize Norton or start a high-level routing back to RAF Waddington (in the case of the Sentinel, Rivet Joint and Sentry). In truth, the shorter the amount of time we kept these aircraft at low level the better. Other than the Hercules and Atlas, they weren't particularly well-suited to flight in the low-level environment and with higher risks of events such as bird-strikes, the quicker we could get them high and out of the way the better. The initial plan had all of these aircraft routing south of Heathrow and entering three holding patterns in a clear area of airspace to the south of Bristol and Brize Norton. The idea was that once all of the other aircraft were completely clear, Air Traffic Control would be able to start vectoring the individual aircraft for recovery. There was debate as to whether we actually needed to have these recovery holding patterns, but at this stage it was better to factor them in rather than not. In terms of the airspace requirement, we would be required to liaise with the operators of Salisbury Plain, an Army range which sat immediately below our holding areas. This would ensure that there wasn't live gun firing or other activity going on if we started stacking aircraft immediately above. The aircraft could still be relatively low so this agreement would be vital. Once the aircraft had started their climb into these areas, we could end the requirement for the Restricted Airspace as Air Traffic Control would then be able to manage them when at height.

This now left the fast-jet formations. There were already twelve egress lines on the map representing the twelve individual formations we had planned thus far and it was starting to look busy. We still had a further seven lines to input. More importantly, these seven lines represented fifty-three aircraft. Either side of these lines, enough space needed to be made available laterally to be able to split apart each formation should they encounter weather and need to climb early. They would of course need to climb at some point depending on where they would be recovering to, but this could be planned further west as the airspace restrictions above their route diminished.

With all previous flypasts I had been involved in, we had avoided London Heathrow as best we could in order to minimise the impact to them. But with the number of aircraft that would need to travel past, an idea occurred that would possibly give something back to Heathrow for the short period of disruption that would inevitably take place. Heathrow sits due west of the Palace by 12 miles. With previous Queen's Birthday Flypasts, we normally routed all of our flypast aircraft to the north of the airport by a few miles thereby avoiding direct overflight of it. This time however, we wondered whether we could actually overfly it. Straight down the length of one of their runways. It would ease our exit from Central London, actually enable our egress to be a little quicker, be simpler for Air Traffic Control and could, we thought, provide a PR opportunity for the UK's biggest airport. With the amount of aircraft we needed to egress, it would also provide a further egress lane for our aircraft to travel through. We hoped that the CAA and airport authorities would go for the idea. It would need a further level of negotiation over and above the general airspace discussions we were having with the stakeholders and the outcome was far from certain. If we could route the fast-jet formations directly down the length of one of the runways, the seven formations could split afterwards. The spectacle of routing aircraft down the main runway of Heathrow was an exciting thought but would mean the pilots hanging on just a bit longer in their formation positions. For the pilots flying the formations, it would also mean a 22-degree turn onto heading post the Palace, and we just weren't sure whether the large '100' formation would be able to crack it and line up perfectly. This would need to be assessed in due course.

With the possibility of overflying Heathrow opening up – subject to the airport authority and CAA approval – both Hawk formations, Tornado, Typhoon, Lightnings and Red Arrows could start their split afterwards. With a split between all of the formations planned as well as speed increases for those aircraft at the front, we could allocate a block of airspace which would encompass this initial plan. As the aircraft climbed out of the low-level environment, they would no longer need the protection of the Restricted Airspace and Air Traffic Control would be able to guide them should anything become an issue. It was quite simplistic at this stage and it would come back later on to cause us problems, but I was content that we had what we needed. The formation route lines on the map were terminated back at all of the formations recovery airfields and with that meant we were now ready to start the detailed discussion with the CAA.

By this point the initial plan was done. Now I've written this down, it seems in hindsight quite a long time to get to a position where we had an initial outlay of what the flypast would look like. It had been over eight months from starting to look at it. Of course, the project was not worked on every day, or even every week, but had to be fitted in among the standard workings of my day job within the Force Headquarters. What took the time was gaining agreements and corresponding with Groups, other Force Headquarters and squadrons against a task that seemed (and was, relatively) a long time away. Many of the units that were to participate in the flypast were also deployed during this period, so there could be significant amounts of time to get a response back to allow the next stage in planning to progress. But it was essential to get to this position as soon as we could. But, by July 2017, the outline plan, with formations and numbers primarily to inform the airspace requirements was known. I wasn't 100 per cent content with the holding patterns and how each formation would enter and depart and knew that there would be a certain amount of movement to optimise the plan, but it would be enough to further the meaningful liaison with the CAA to gain our required Restricted Airspace. The basic egress plan would also change as planning evolved but again it was sufficient at this stage. There were also a lot of moving parts in terms of aircraft forward deploying to non-home base locations and in the background each of the formation leaders were

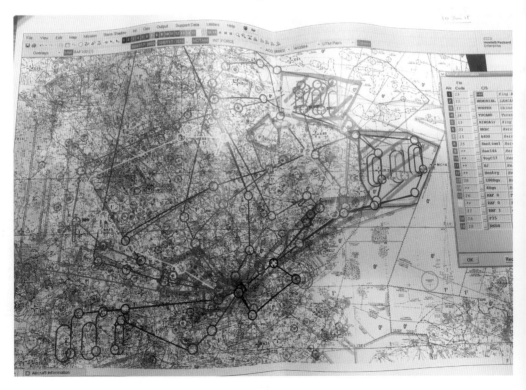

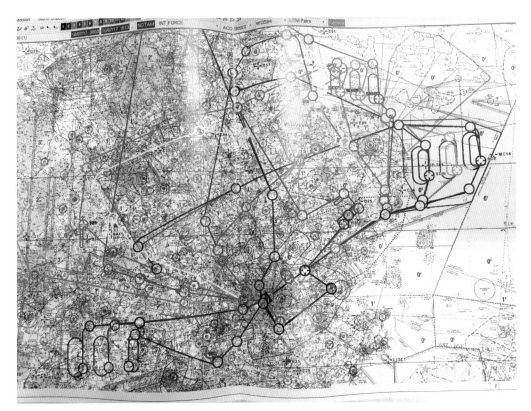

Early mission-planning maps showing the initial extent of the formations, holds, ingress and egress routing. The blue boxes show my initial workings of what I thought we would need in terms of airspace provision. I also still had the Dakota leading the formation at this stage – something which changed later on in the planning process. (© *Crown Copyright 2018, Wg Cdr Kevin Gatland*)

liaising with their respective bases to ensure success on the day. In addition to this our Force Commander, my immediate boss, was to move on in September 2017 to start a Staff course. My job was about to get busier both in terms of managing the office on a day-to-day basis, but also it meant that our discussions on delivering the flypast would need to route via a different person. We would still formally have a Force Commander to replace Steve Ward but they wouldn't be sat in the office with me on a daily basis.

## Chapter 4

# Twelve Months and Counting

With about a year to go, all the concepts were there but I knew that the size of this event would demand an exceptional team to ensure it all came together. Once airborne, each formation would be individually responsible on the day for executing the flypast, but it would need a small team of people prior to ensure that the skeleton plan we had thus far would develop into a fully-fledged and successful flypast. Suffice to say failure simply was not an option. With the posting of Group Captain Steve Ward to a Staff course, I had started routing the plans and ideas as they developed via Group Captain Jonny Moreton, the Senior Air Staff Officer who sat within No. 1 Group at High Wycombe. With better access to Air Vice Marshal Gerry Mayhew, the Flypast Senior Responsible Officer, Jonny was able to continue filtering and advising the intent of the senior hierarchy. It also stopped any of my crazy ideas going any further! This arrangement, with video teleconferencing briefings at least monthly, and many phone calls and emails, worked well but was focused looking up. The PowerPoint slides, papers and skeleton plan now needed to be transposed into an accurate sortie profile for each aircraft type and formation that they could fly on the day. I now needed a more tactical working group to further develop the plan with a mind to those who would actually be flying it.

Growing a new team of people brings both a degree of additional complexity but more importantly capacity. It also allowed a wider range of additional ideas, questions and contingency considerations to be brought into the mix. Two (or in our case, multiple) heads are definitely better than one. Much of the plan would need to be developed with the flying crews remotely and at range, as nearly all of the aircraft would take off from different bases being spread across the UK. There were discussions as to who would be best placed to assist me in planning. Options ranged from whether it would be better having someone from the helicopter force, multi-engine fleet or the Typhoons, but ultimately the simplest option was a pair of Tornado aircrew from my home-base at RAF Marham. Thankfully, there was a ready supply of aircrew willing to take on this role.

We needed highly experienced aircrew who could intricately understand the complex issues of bringing together the event. The two selected chaps were Squadron Leader Matt Axcell and Squadron Leader Mahmoud Abdallah, both from 31 Squadron. Their task would be to work alongside me in generating the final sortie plan. There was a critical liaison role between us and the rest of the formation leaders, which at this stage were starting to move from discussions with the other element Force Headquarters and into the squadrons and to the pilots which would actually participate. We would also need to continually adjust the plan dependent on any subsequent changes which were made, be it from the RAF's hierarchy or operational demands, through to changes in aircraft numbers and formations.

A plan wouldn't be a complete plan, however, without the expertise brought in by Air Traffic Control. While having flown over 2,000 hours myself, the intricacies of managing aircraft from a console were a world apart. Banter between aircrew and air traffic controllers (occasionally called the flying prevention branch) is always high and generally jovial but experience has shown that their knowledge can make or break a plan and I needed them in full-time from this point onwards. While the previous work had not been done in isolation, the inclusion of professional controllers was paramount. It had been something we had identified repeatedly over previous flypast events and I sought to bring in the controllers that would actually be working on the day. That way, the ownership and understanding of the plan would be integral to them, which would have the benefit of them being aware of all of the nuances of what we would be seeking to achieve. It would also, hopefully mean, less reactive management would be required as the controllers also had complete awareness of the plan.

I was glad to have Squadron Leader Lorraine Hawthorn and Warrant Officer Mel Young on the team to deliver this. Situated in the National Air Traffic Services building at Swanwick, to the south-east of Southampton, the Air Traffic Control elements of the flypast would be coordinated and run from there on the day. If there was one area where you do not want poor coordination and lack of understanding, it would be within the team controlling the air traffic. The finest plans are almost always altered once they are enacted and it would be no different with this one. But with detailed understanding and close cooperation, any negative effects could be minimised. The controllers sat in Swanwick would also be sat next to their civilian counterparts so the cooperation extended beyond just the military planning and execution of the event.

Air traffic management goes hand in hand with the airspace required. Now having worked on producing the Queen's Birthday Flypast which occurred in the June, we had, over the course of the year, built up a book of contacts to smooth the way. Rob Gratton and Matt Lee were my go-to men in the CAA and were absolutely essential in advising on how we would go about gaining the airspace that we would require. Critically, they also were the link between us in the military and the civilian airports and other civilian airspace users who we would be affecting. It was to them that I first addressed the plans and airspace requirements that had been put together over the previous eight months. If their answer was no, it may well see us going back to the drawing board.

Gaining agreement to shut down huge portions of UK airspace is no mean feat and is ultimately authorised by the Department for Transport. One of the main issues, as can be imagined, is that for our flypast to occur safely, all air traffic would need to cease departing and landing into London's very busy Heathrow and City airports for a period of time. The route of the flypast meant that safe separation between the flights and the flypast aircraft could not be guaranteed otherwise. The amount of time that Heathrow and City would need to hold operations would depend on their runway in use on the day as well as the routing that all of our aircraft would take. With flights taking off and landing into Heathrow almost continuously, it was obvious that we should try to minimise the effect of the flypast on them. London City was not too problematic as the flypast would route about 5 miles north and would not get any closer. However, for Heathrow this was a completely different story. While normally we would route around Heathrow, the plan had us routing straight through the overhead. From the first initial discussion, a number of meetings held in CAA House in London, as well as at Heathrow airport itself, began.

The purpose of all of the meetings was two-fold. First, to gain agreement on the use of the entire block of airspace and then to understand the totality of the impact on the UKs busiest airport, and second, whether our Heathrow overflight proposal could be agreed. For the airport authorities, it would also mean discussions with the airlines as to how their schedules would be affected. It was all these factors that drove our requirement to speak to them as soon as feasibly possible.

To achieve all of this, the expertise of Rob Gratton and Matt Lee were paramount. We spent some time reviewing and revising our airspace plan. Detailed examination of the initial plans required of the airspace yielded airspace areas which we could afford to hand back, as well as other areas where we would want to expand – even if we weren't using that exact portion. All aspects of the plan were driven with safety in mind and this included the airspace plan. While we had a sketch map of what was the minimum required, consideration was given to how this would actually affect airspace users on the day. As an example, we ended up expanding some areas to avoid a potential funnelling of aircraft through various routes. This would happen where we had Restricted Airspace either side and then a gap down the centre. I thought initially having gaps would be a better plan of action as it could allow access to a small airfield, thereby reducing the impact to general aviation. But, from their experience, this could be problematic. Murphy's Law occurs here – if it can go wrong it will do, and allowing a narrow corridor between two areas of Restricted Airspace is almost an invitation to an inadvertent airspace infringement and may also act as a temptation to legally fly light aircraft into a position to observe the flypast. By closing down these areas, it firstly removed the possibility of an infringement, which was good for everyone, including the general aviation pilot and secondly, would allow us slightly more scope for manoeuvre as the plan progressed. For the crews flying, it also meant that they would be far less likely to see non-participating aircraft very close to their route which could give cause for concern.

We also looked in detail over timings and which blocks of airspace could become active and when. The area was so huge that it would not make sense if it were all active at the same time, but thankfully because the time over the Palace was fixed, we could afford to be very accurate with area activation and deactivation times. Due to this fixed time, there was very little variance required, and aircraft would either leave the holding areas on time or not at all. There was no scope to allow 'catch-up' if they missed their slot time – there were simply too many other aircraft and formations ahead and behind.

Over time, the airspace plan was subtly amended to a point where it needed to be submitted through the statutory and legislative process to gain approval. The areas of the airspace were broken to nine and each allocated with a lower and upper height, and activation and deactivation times. Once we had achieved this and it was submitted, there were no more amendments. Times and dimensions were fixed. These were predicated on the final outcome of the flypast planning and Air Traffic Control inputs.

With our full understanding of the airspace and timings, our engagement with the London airports and the CAA continued. Behind the scenes at their end, Heathrow assessed in detail the level of disruption that would occur. There were some things that they could phase in which needed to be done anyway. As an example, a runway sweep was a mandatory item that was normally carried out during the day at particular points and took around five minutes. If this was scheduled in during the time when the flypast would be occurring, it would free five minutes elsewhere and therefore help with the departure and recovery scheduling. With every minute being vital to Heathrow's output, this sort of event scheduling was critical. My main role was keeping them updated with any changes to the plan as it developed, as well as attending and briefing at any pertinent meetings. Following a number of meetings with the CAA, London airports, the SRO Gerry Mayhew and myself, we gained agreement to the overflight proposal. Overflight of the northern-most runway was chosen. The particular operation on the day would depend on which runway was in use at the time. For westerly departures (i.e. Runway 27), the last departure would need to be rolling no later than 1200 hrs, i.e. the same time that *Vortex* were over the Palace. Departures could then recommence once the flypast aircraft were clear of the departure tracks. This would be around 1213 giving a total stop time of thirteen minutes. For aircraft arriving, the stop time would be longer at seventeen minutes. The last arrival could land no later than 1201 hrs with the next arrival being scheduled to be at a twelve-mile final approach by no earlier than 1213 hrs, landing at 1217 hrs.

Should Heathrow be on the easterly runways (Runway 09), the stops would need to be greater. The last departing aircraft would need to roll by 1154 hrs and departures could then recommence again at 1213 hrs giving a stop time of nineteen minutes. The last arriving aircraft would need to land no later than 1155 hrs. Arrivals could recommence with the first aircraft on a long final at 12 miles by 1214 hrs, landing at 1218hrs. The total stop time in this case was twenty-three minutes.

Following this understanding of how Heathrow would operate and with another planning milestone now agreed, the intricacies of the flypast planning could continue.

## Additional Overflight Locations

It was during this time of detailed planning that the ideas of adding in additional overflight locations of either National or military significance were decided. While the Palace would obviously remain our prime focus, with the weight of effort that was going into the day it seemed nonsensical to disregard any other opportunities. We had incorporated Heathrow already but a further overflight location was staring us in the face and its incorporation would be convenient as well as ease the routing for the flypast post-Heathrow.

Windsor Castle, with its pre-eminent position sitting atop a hill some 5 miles due west of Heathrow airport, has long been a Royal residence. Normally military aircraft need to avoid this location, but it was worth asking whether we would indeed be able to overfly it on this special day. The position of the Castle allowed us to continue the straight line track of the flypast from Heathrow before we started to turn the aircraft and formations to break them apart from each other. The total height of the Castle was just over 350ft above sea level so we would need to factor that in to our planning and overflight heights but providing we obtained the relevant permissions, this location seemed like a good choice as an additional location.

The other two locations which we had ideas for and planned to overfly were the RAF Museum at Hendon and the RAF Memorial at Runnymede. Both did not require specific approval as Windsor Castle did, and we thought it very appropriate that if we could, we should overfly these locations as well. As with all of the additional locations, once we started the detail of the intricate planning, they lent themselves very much to particular formations with little issue. The slower formations of the Prefects (callsign *Warboys*), Tucanos (callsign *Swift*) and Shadows (callsign *Snake*) would already be exiting to the north after overflying the Palace so routing them over Hendon was simple and the obvious choice. As was the routing for the heavy aircraft (*Snapshot* – Sentinel, *Tartan* – Voyager, *Goose* – Rivet Joint and *Sentry* – E-3D) to pass over Runnymede. The fast-jet Hawks (*Aggressor* and *Ninja*), Tornados (*Monster*), F-35s (*Gibson*), Typhoon (*Cobra*, *Triplex*, *Warlord*) and Red Arrows (*Red Arrows*) were left to overfly Heathrow and Windsor Castle. By having these additional locations, it aided us with the deconfliction plan in many respects. As all of the aircraft were already at their minimum time-spacing criteria by the time they flew over the Palace, they needed to start splitting up anyway and it also meant that only co-speed aircraft could continue following each other to each location. If not, we would have had faster formations overtaking slower formations and that was something we had to avoid. The natural split in these locations meant that we had started breaking the whole formation apart into a number of smaller elements.

There were, of course, a number of other worthy places to have tried to route the formation over and much could be, and has been, said of the flypast being very London-focused; however, the coordination levels needed were immense and importantly, fuel was always an issue. It would have been fantastic to have done more but it was simply not a realistic option.

One aspect that I hadn't appreciated early on in the flypast planning was that The Championships at Wimbledon would be occurring at the same time. As it happened and by chance, the initial egress lines of *Dakota* and *Memorial* were planned to go almost directly overhead. This was not intentional as it had been a route planned by timing and deconfliction rather than anything else. However, on realising both events would be occurring on the day and sensing an opportunity, we enquired as to whether Wimbledon would like the aircraft to route directly overhead. We could give accurate timings and it would have given some additional media coverage. The initial response looked promising but ultimately the organisers decided against it. We had to revert to keeping comfortably clear with a slight reroute; it was a shame but it would have been something of an interruption during the middle of a match!

## The 100 Centre-Piece

While I can't remember exactly when the '100' centrepiece was finally changed, the make-up of the '100' had been a continual discussion point. While we had decided initially that it would be a mix of Tornado and Typhoon aircraft, through the detailed planning phase there was potentially a better option emerging. Twenty-six aircraft in the formation was proving a challenging burden. The option to slightly downscale was made. Now a total of twenty-two aircraft could make up the '100' and it was decided that it could all be completed by one aircraft type, the Typhoon. It seemed simpler and also allowed the Tornados to form an additional formation immediately behind. Because only the Typhoon Force would conduct it, training issues would be reduced and the delivery of the '100' could be completed in-house. It freed up the Tornado and with it being the Tornado Force's final year due to its out-of-service date in March 2019, a standalone formation was seen as a better send-off than being the smaller part of a larger formation.

It also meant that I needed a non-Marham based sub-project manager of just that formation. Airborne, it would be led by Wing Commander Andy Chisholm, a very experienced and capable pilot and squadron commander of 29(R). Being a busy squadron commander and knowing that it would require significant prior planning, a small team led by Squadron Leader Mike Childs set to work to manage the intricacies of delivering this large formation. There were so many aspects to consider. Planning for this formation began in earnest in October 2017. An ex-Red Arrows pilot, Mike's aim was to deliver a safe and feasible plan for the formation which would allow them to slot into the formation position allocated. The challenges were immense. RAF Coningsby was to be the take-off and landing location but this would still require a whole Force effort, with assistance being given from the squadrons at their sister base of RAF Lossiemouth. They would plan to detach six aircraft and pilots for a period of three weeks immediately prior to the 10 July. From an engineering perspective this required new procedures and ways of working to be generated. The aircraft parking areas at Coningsby would be full of aircraft and there needed to be sufficient spares, tools and test equipment to be immediately available. It was to prove a very busy time for them, in addition to maintaining their other commitments around the world, as well as holding the UK's Quick Reaction Alert posture continuously.

The delivery of the Typhoon '100' came in two main parts. The first was in managing how the actual formation would fly together once it was airborne. This required new standard operating procedures as well as looking at new reference positions to ensure that the formation looked like a perfect '100' from the ground, as well as maintaining all elements of safety. The second part was in the planning aspects of getting the whole formation airborne, into the holds, into and then out of the '100' position, egress and then finally, the recovery. It wouldn't be over until the last aircraft landed and shut down.

To manage the first part, Mike and the team measured all of the possible dimensions required. Not just the width and length of the Typhoon itself, but also every distance involved between each of the aircraft as well as between each of the three individual formation elements. Drawn on a whiteboard and paced out on the ground at Coningsby to show the new formation positions, various adaptations were made. It turned out that 85 metres was required between the outside and centre '0', with 64 metres required between the '1' and the inside '0'. These dimensions were between the lead elements of those formations and as such would leave an equal gap of 33 metres between the closest two Typhoons further back in the formation. The total length and width of the formation needed to be carefully considered to ensure that the formation did not look either too wide or narrow, long or short. Each aircraft was also slightly stepped down as it went further to the rear of the formation. They would naturally want to do this anyway to avoid sitting in the jet efflux of the one in front but it was also to try to present a better image of the '100' as it approached. Evidently, airborne practice and amendment would be required to ensure that it looked just right and this was to come in the three weeks prior to the main event.

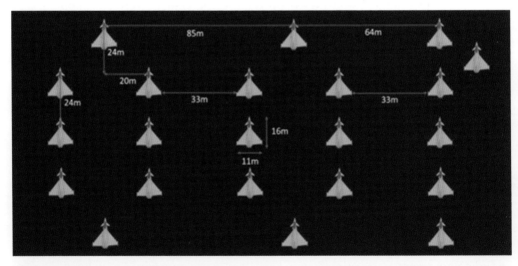

Measuring distances relative to each aircraft allowed us to understand the total width of the formation as well as ensure that there were adequate distances between each aircraft and element. These were combined with suitable references to enable all of the pilots to fly an accurate formation reference on each other.

The second-half of the planning focused on how we would get the formation safely out of Coningsby, into the hold, then join it together before it was then split apart and recovered back to Coningsby after the flypast. With limited fuel carried in each Typhoon, one very important aspect was to ensure that they could get off the ground as quickly as possible and not spend any more time holding than necessary. Each drop of fuel was vital and this would be critical in ensuring a successful recovery of all of the aircraft back in to Coningsby.

There are a few ways of getting large numbers of aircraft off the runway in short succession. The team decided that a short stream take-off would be most efficient and they allocated themselves a seven-minute window to get all of the aircraft up. It wasn't just twenty-two aircraft however. Spare aircraft and 'whip' aircraft (an aircraft which whips the formation into shape, often by flying above and directing slight position amendments) were needed which brought the total to twenty-six. To maximise efficiency, this would require that each of the core flypast aircraft were separated in a twenty second stream – one behind the other. Unlike the Tornado, which needed time for engine parameters to be noted down at max dry power on the runway, the Typhoon could roll straight on to the runway and depart immediately. This significantly eased the required time on the runway for all of the aircraft and those following. Once airborne, the long stream of aircraft would remain low and make their way towards their respective hold north of the North Norfolk coast, ideally maintaining radar or visual contact with the one ahead. Once all of the aircraft in each individual element were together in the hold, the formation could start to loosely join into their respective '1' or '0'. The formation would not tighten right up until much closer to London. They would all plan to leave the holds at about the same time, heading southbound on separate routes which would then slowly converge bringing the three elements together. It would therefore allow each element to settle into their formation before combining as one. Once the call had been made to bring the '100' together, the centre '0', callsign *Triplex*, would form first. Following that, the second '0', callsign *Warlord*, would form next, with the '1', callsign *Cobra*, forming last. There were very specific procedures that each of the elements would follow to get themselves into the formation references previously described. Each of the individual aircraft would start from a well-known standard formation position before starting their move. For the '0' for example, the front three aircraft would be already flying in a three-ship vic with a pair behind in echelon and the rear three in vic. When commanded, the centre two aircraft would move apart and into respective line astern positions behind the front aircraft, which would then allow the rear three to close up and form the final part of the '0'. There is nothing complicated here but it was completed in exactly the same way, with the same radio calls each time. While simple, there were still eight fast-jet aircraft manoeuvring around each other with other feet to spare. Everyone had to know exactly what the procedures were.

With the initial idea of placing all of the '100' participants in the North Norfolk coast holds, the main challenge we had then was how we would get the whole formation onto the correct run-in line. We looked at multiple options for the Typhoon routing including whether we could place some elements in the Southwold hold, or keep the formation wider, or indeed much narrower. We looked at oversea routes from the hold, so bringing them down the east coast past Norwich, or southbound overland to the west of Norwich. Both had advantages and disadvantages and it was always going to be a compromise. Ultimately, we needed to be able to swing all of the aircraft through some 90 degrees to get them onto the right heading. Routing aircraft oversea past Norwich would have reduced the disruption to general aviation operating overland, but it took additional fuel and also meant a number of large heading changes. The heading changes were manageable but having aircraft flowing through what should be empty holds, led to potential confliction problems if aircraft had remained there due to serviceability issues. On balance, the decision to route the '100' southbound and overland was by far the better option. But with a large turn near Ipswich this meant that the '100' would not be fully formed until they were heading inbound to London. Their timing also had to be impeccable. Directly ahead would be the Tornado and F-35 formations while immediately behind would be the Red Arrows. Those aircraft as well would need to be spot on with their timings or there could be a real confliction issue as they all closed towards each other to form the line of aircraft. Being co-speed, there was just thirty seconds between them so they needed to operate within the prescriptive tolerance of plus or minus five seconds, as well as being on their flypast speed to stay within our safety limits. Managing all of this required a great degree of skill.

The greatest challenge for the '100' formation was not in the ingress, however, but lay in the egress phase. No one had the experience of dealing with twenty-two aircraft in very close formation, let alone how we would safely split them apart to recover them back to a single airfield. We needed a robust plan which catered for not only the intricacies of splitting up the formation, but also doing it cognizant of poor weather and under what could be a relatively low and thick cloud-base. They may well find themselves in the position where the cloud-base was completely fit and legal for the 1,000-foot flypast, but then thick cloud was stacked from 2,000ft upwards. This would present a challenge in that the Typhoons would have to separate into much smaller elements at low level, before climbing under instrument meteorological conditions until they broke cloud high above. This could simply not be done in the size of units they would be in. They had to be broken into much smaller sections. To do this effectively takes some time, distance and space. Once they were finally established at height, they would then need to negotiate the airways which run north to south down the centre of the UK before starting their descent back into Coningsby to land. It wasn't finished until every single aircraft was on the deck. On a normal good weather day, most fast-jet aircraft perform an airfield recovery called a Visual Run-in and Break –

essentially a high-speed pass (around 420 knots) down the centre of the runway in use before banking hard left or right onto the reciprocal heading, bleeding off the speed downwind to enable the lowering of flaps and landing gear. The final turn in would then align them with the in-use runway in order to land. It was a very efficient way of getting a lot of aircraft down in one go and required minimal Air Traffic Control help, but does rely on good weather. We hoped for this but had to cater for the other eventuality. If the weather was poor, each aircraft would need to perform an instrument-based landing, either a formal Instrument Landing System (ILS) approach, similar to an airliner, or a set-up on the Precision Approach Radar (PAR). Both options severely limited the amount of aircraft which could recover at any one time. We had to cater for the worst-case scenario. The only option was to separate the formation sufficiently through time. We therefore had to start planning the recovery from the moment that the Typhoons had overflown Heathrow airport. They would need a lot of space and we spent some considerable time ensuring that we could generate a suitable split in order to assist with this. The first section of this, split the three individual elements apart – a reverse of what we had done on the ingress. Simultaneously, speed differentials could be used to then separate the individual '1', '0' and '0' into smaller elements. The elements could then start to climb. This climb could not be done too early as on the egress there was still a lot of controlled airspace above – airspace that we did not have as part of our bespoke Restricted Airspace. This did not matter too much as we would need 30–40 miles or so to ensure the split occurred successfully. Andy Chisholm as the overall airborne lead, as well as the individual element leaders, would also have to assess the weather on the day to take the best course of action, but the plan would help enable this. Once they were up at height, and as with the heavy aircraft, a couple of holding locations were built into the plan before the Typhoons crossed the major north/south airways. This was done to ensure Air Traffic Control and the Typhoons had a pre-defined option to hold if required. Once we had planned all of this out, the mission-planning software showed, as a real-time fly-through, how it would all look. After much juggling of speeds, waypoint locations and climb heights, we finally had a fully deconflicted plan which spaced the aircraft out well for recovery. The final piece of the jigsaw was to cater for the contingency of what would happen if one of the Typhoons crashed or had a major incident on recovery. The worst case was that it would be the first aircraft to land. The remaining aircraft would all then need to divert or hold sufficiently long for the issue to be resolved. For this, each segment of the '100' had a different diversion airfield to split the load.

Notwithstanding the challenges of the Typhoon '100' formation as a sub-project, Matt and Mo had continued their sterling job dealing with the continual flow of minor and major changes as they arose. February and March of 2018 were particularly busy with much of the intricate planning being completed at squadron level. Meetings were held at RAF Brize Norton to cover 10, 47, 70 and 99 Squadrons as well as the Operations centre there, and the same happened in March at Waddington for 5, 8, 14 and 51 Squadrons. On 13 March, 72 and 100 Squadron visited Marham, with 28 Squadron following on 21 March. The purpose of all of these meetings was to try to ratify the planning aspects which had often been done remotely or over the phone or by email. Individual plans were sent out for formation leads to assess but as is often the case, once a plan is seen in context, surrounded by all of the other participants, it needs an amendment. The problem was that each time this happened it would almost certainly affect another formation. This would then require further dialogue to resolve the confliction issues that were nearly always generated. We found out that the 100 Squadron Hawks would not be able to return to Leeming due to their limited fuel loads so they needed a new landing option, which we resolved as being Boscombe Down, and their original holding location and routing changed completely. We lost aircraft as the planning progressed as well, which again often necessitated changes in set-up, or take-off and landing location, or hold and route. Rarely was it simple. The planned King Air formation was removed as we learnt that their out-of-service date was now March 2018 and the dynamics of the heavy aircraft fleet and their commitments and serviceability meant that we ended up dropping down to single aircraft rather than the four (or other multiples) planned. While understandable and out-with anyone's control, it was disappointing not to be able to showcase the multiple large aircraft in formation. It is, and was, incredibly rare to see four Hercules in formation, let alone four Atlas as well. Sadly, it was not to be for this flypast either. The original ten Chinook formation reduced to six due to their commitment to Mali taking priority. As aircraft dropped out, we sought other options to ensure we kept the total numbers up at one hundred. The fruition of the original option of adding in the new Juno and Jupiter helicopters as well as the Prefect aircraft was a very welcome surprise and, being brand new aircraft in the inventory, demonstrated the future of the Royal Air Force in its aircrew training capacity. We were still denied the use of the new Phenom and Texan.

All parts of the plan went through a continual process of iterative improvement. The fundamentals remained, but combining the inputs from Lorraine and Mel who were leading the air traffic management along with Matt and Mo meant a number of changes. There were other minor amendments such as renaming the holds in the order that aircraft would leave them which assisted air traffic management. Squawks (a code allocated to each aircraft which would show up on the air traffic radar screen) were sequentially numbered to provide clarity against each aircraft and a system of control frequencies were allocated to provide a manageable and effective way of talking to over one hundred aircraft. I believe our total frequencies used was around fifty. Each hold had a separate frequency which allowed aircraft to communicate discretely with other aircraft in the hold as well. There was then a primary and secondary frequency for the main aspect of the flypast and crews were only allowed to switch across to this frequency at a particular geographic point. Each formation had a discrete frequency allocated to it to allow them to talk intra-formation as well. This all required management and due to the numbers of aircraft, new operating procedures were introduced specifically for the flypast. With so many aircraft eventually ending up on one frequency – Flypast Primary – we needed to ensure that it didn't become saturated with radio communications. Normally, when an aircraft checks in to a new frequency there is a standard list of information that is passed between aircraft and Air Traffic Control. It also includes a number of standard phrases such as 'aircraft are responsible for their own terrain clearance'. We decided early on that to do this each time an aircraft checked in to the frequency would be vastly inefficient and detrimentally clog up the radio so we decided that we could eliminate some of this excess communication by briefing it on the ground and therefore limiting the communication flow to other essential and safety items only. Efficiency was the aim of the game which ultimately enhanced safety.

Continuing with the iterative improvements, we moved aircraft around between the holds to optimise which formation should go where and a main consideration was always how much fuel was carried. Thankfully, the holding patterns and aircraft allocation did not change too markedly. The Battle of Britain Memorial Flight take off location shifted from Southend to RAF Waddington, but this change was offset by a change to their recovery routing post the Palace and subsequent landing at RAF Fairford and Southampton. *Ninja*, the IV Squadron Hawks, also changed their landing location to RAF Odiham due to fuel concerns. The real significance of all of these changes lay in the deconfliction of the egress routing. While we could fan the formations out as best we could, we still had a large amount of aircraft in a relatively small piece of sky. Again, every single time a route changed it impacted on the other routes and a slight adjustment would be made to ensure that the formations of aircraft remained deconflicted from each other. We ensured there was sufficient space to spread out to allow them to start their climb to higher levels to return to their bases.

It was noted earlier that the heavy package was routed via the Runnymede Memorial which, as they were all co-speed, meant that we could keep their package together in thirty-second intervals. This routing also kept them comfortably clear of all of the other aircraft egressing. Our concerns at this stage were in the recovery phase back to Brize Norton. As the total numbers of heavy aircraft reduced it would ease the burden, but there was always the slim possibility of more large aircraft being available so we determined that we would retain the separate recovery holds to put them into should we need them. There was a high likelihood that they would not be needed as the air traffic controllers expected to be able to sequence the aircraft in normally, but it would be worth having a planned contingency measure in case. If on the day, Brize Norton Air Traffic Control did not need them, then they could go unused with no impact.

As the planning started its inevitable conclusion as the 10th approached, the intensity increased and with it our continual search for betterment across all elements of the plan. In addition to the agreement for the Restricted Airspace, we also needed to ensure we had overflight permissions for the various danger areas that we would need to overfly. Overall risk assessment remained ongoing, certainly in gaining the required paperwork against the single-engine overflight risk. In twelve months, much had changed but, thankfully, much had stayed the same. It was pleasing to see that many of our initial assumptions had stood the test of time and as planning focused in more and more as July approached the team had continued their excellent work. In the immediate weeks prior, we had a full formation list – we had to try to go as firm on this as early as possible as media attention, written pieces, flying suit patches and badges, t-shirts and other memorabilia had all needed to be printed. Even then we still had a few last-minute changes which did not make it. The final constitution of the Battle of Britain Memorial aircraft would keep changing right until the final day and, of course, at this stage we had planned for delivery of an exact one-hundred-aircraft flypast over the flypast and Palace. Our final design to be briefed was as follows:

| | |
|---|---|
| First Formation | *Vortex*; 3 x Puma leading 6 x Chinook |
| Second formation | *Spectre*; 2 x Juno leading 1 Jupiter |
| Third formation | *Dakota*; 1 x DC-3 |
| Fourth formation | *Memorial*; 1 x Lancaster leading 1 x Hurricane and 4 x Spitfire |
| Fifth formation | *Warboys*; 3 x Prefect |
| Sixth formation | *Swift*; 9 x Tucano |
| Seventh formation | *Snake*; 2 x Shadow |
| Eighth formation | *Zorro*; 1 x Hercules |
| Ninth formation | *Grizzly*; 1 x A400M |
| Tenth formation | *Blackcat*; 1 x C17 leading 1 x BAe 146 |
| Eleventh formation | *Snapshot*; 1 x Sentinel |
| Twelfth formation | *Tartan*; 1 x Voyager |
| Thirteenth formation | *Goose*; 1 x Rivet Joint |
| Fourteenth formation | *Sentry*; 1 x E-3D Sentry |
| Fifteenth formation | *Aggressor*; 9 x Hawk |
| Sixteenth formation | *Ninja*; 9 x Hawk |
| Seventeenth formation | *Monster*; 7 x Tornado |
| Eighteenth formation | *Gibson*; 3 x F-35 Lightning |
| Nineteenth formation | *Typhoon* (*Cobra*, *Triplex* and *Warlord*); 22 x Typhoon |
| Twentieth formation | *Red Arrows*; 9 x Hawk |

One of our final tasks was to ensure that we had integrated the airborne media and police helicopters into our plan. This really meant the requests for a BBC and Sky

News helicopter to be airborne in the vicinity to capture footage and pictures for their news networks. We would also have our own A–109 helicopter over London as well as the Police helicopter. We needed to ensure that we deconflicted them from our flypast as well as providing them access to where they needed to go. Our A–109 would act as one of the weather-check helicopters – they would be able to give us very accurate cloud-base heights and would be present throughout the flypast. It would also serve as our photo-helicopter. From previous flypasts we knew that the best position for this was in the overshoot of the Palace. The photographer could then get the great shots that you can see in this book, with the Palace in the background and looking down the Mall. For the remaining three helicopters, we positioned them in three further locations within their own 2-mile circle. All of the helicopters had to maintain at or above 1,900ft. This would ensure that they always remained 500ft clear of any flypast traffic.

## Demonstrating the Flight Planning.

As has been obvious throughout, safety was the paramount feature. Now we had an overall plan and agreed conception of the flypast we needed to be able to demonstrate how the whole thing was going to flow. I've mentioned the mission-planning software previously and it gave us the preferred way of demonstrating how it would all come together. We had incorporated each formation's route from take-off to landing to ensure that the aircraft would be fully deconflicted from each other throughout. This method would also ease the real-time air traffic burden as we could factor their separation requirements into the plan, which would make things far easier on the day. We hadn't gone to this level of detail previously when planning the annual Queen's Birthday Flypasts. Previously, the plans had started from the holding areas and finished as aircraft started to climb out as they egressed from London. This worked as the size had not warranted further levels of coordination and Air Traffic Control had capacity to manage aircraft from take-off to their holds and back again after the flypast. Due to the numbers this time, however, we felt that this additional level of detailed planning would be required. First, it ensured that we had enough Air Traffic Control capacity, i.e. controllers physically sat at consoles, and second, the routes into the holding areas, and more importantly the routing afterwards in the egress phase, were fully deconflicted. Finally, it also ensured that aircraft arrived back at airfields with an appropriate spacing to allow them to recover. This was particularly pertinent for the large numbers of Typhoon aircraft.

Aside from the actual management of the aircraft, there had been a huge amount of paperwork, agreements, authorisations and other tasks to keep on top of. To track all of these moving parts I used a simple but very effective spreadsheet to track the data flows. Spread across a number of horizontal lines, I had broken down each major

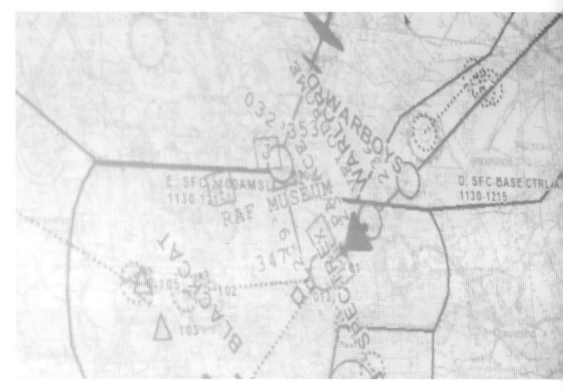

The use of the advanced Mission Planning Aid was critical to the success of the flypast. Every formation could see where it would be flying in relation to the other, as well as how far apart they would be separated at each point. (© *Crown Copyright 2018, Cpl Steve Buckley*)

group of tasks. Along each horizontal line lay another set of sub-tasks and within each of those would consist a number of individual actions. Each task was therefore grouped into a set depending on the grouped task to which it belonged. It wasn't particularly sophisticated and each block was allocated a Red, Amber or Green annotation depending on whether a task was yet to be started, in progress or completed. Some of these would not be fully completed until near the day itself. In all, however, it proved very effective, and combined with me keeping a notepad beside my bed at night to capture midnight thoughts, provided a constructive method of ensuring all tasks, requests and documentation was kept up to date. It also, at a snapshot, allowed me to brief my hierarchy as to exactly what progress had been made and what still needed to be delivered.

While we now had a plan which would deliver a grand flypast, it was still not yet totally complete. Each formation had their individual plan and this plan meshed with all of the other formations taking part. What remained was to ensure that we could cater for as many eventualities as we could. The plan could not fail due to contingencies that we could have planned for and mitigated against.

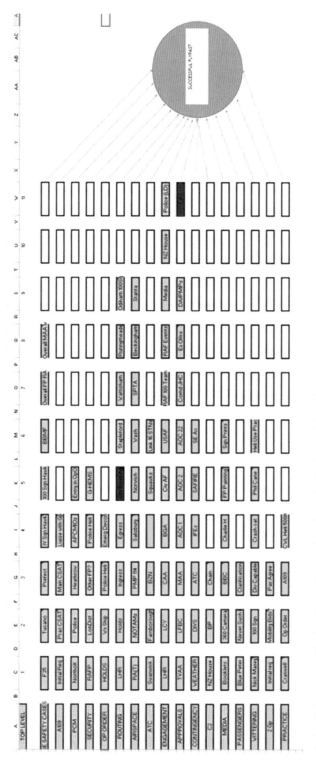

A simple but very effective form of managing the task. Under each heading sat a further list of tasks which needed to be completed. If I hadn't started it, it was red. Once I had commenced the task it turned amber and once fully completed it was green. At a glance I could see what still needed to be done without worrying I'd miss anything. The tracker grew as the months went on.

*Chapter 5*

# Contingency – Planning for the 'What Ifs?'

At the heart of all military flying is being able to plan and cater for as many 'What Ifs?' as possible, having thought about what could go wrong during a sortie or event and then having thought through a remedy which would mitigate, or even better negate, that event occurring in the first place. In every military sortie that is flown, the pre-flight briefing would have included an element of discussion about undesirable events. These may include take-off emergencies, poor weather and encountering various equipment failures. Many of these issues would have standard operating procedures which all crews would be aware of in how to deal with the issue. For specific sortie types, any unusual risks or issues would be specifically talked through with the aim of providing a resolution to mitigate or eliminate the issue. The flypast was certainly no different and, in this regard, planning contingencies for the flypast held some similarities to contingency planning for the large exercises we had flown in over our careers, whether it be an eighty-aircraft Red Flag exercise in the United States, or a sixty-aircraft European Tactical Leadership Programme training mission. The concept was always the same – think of the issues, plan a response to that issue. Just the concept of having thought about a potential problem prior to its occurrence lessens the impact of it and provides your brain with a rapid option once airborne should it materialise.

The main difference here was that under nearly all other circumstances, large missions such as these would be operating either in a war-zone or, more likely, in a large sanitised block of airspace well away from large populations, cities and towns. We would be doing completely the opposite. We would also be doing this under the constraint of remaining inside our Restricted Airspace as much as possible. The contingency planning had to take all of these elements into account and cater for it. Contingency options were never far from our minds throughout the planning process and started as soon as we began to look at the airspace design. Having holding areas over the sea mitigated the impact on civilian operations as best we could as well as provided areas where we were unlikely to meet any other traffic. Fuel-efficient forward-operating locations gave greater flexibility for formations to manage their fuel on the day and, as previously mentioned, we ensured the airspace was built with as few problematic 'funnels' as possible and had sufficient space either side of the flypast 'centre-line'. This basic level of safety and contingency was built in before detailed planning began. Always with a mind to these aspects, this process continued as the plan developed.

Aside from the physical aspects of the plan and where aircraft were to be located, we brain-stormed a list of all possible scenarios as broad and unlikely as we could imagine. From the obvious such as poor and changeable weather conditions, to the extreme, such as a terrorist attack on the aircraft with a shoulder-launched missile launched from inside Central London. Each scenario was examined and then we attempted to put the most appropriate response in place. We did this in conjunction with the post-crash management team who also worked alongside the Gold, Silver and Bronze commanders in the Met Police who ultimately would be controlling the ground scenario on the day. The reality was that there was not much we could do once an aircraft had crashed, as the process would then be outwith our control. On the day, it would be handled by the emergency services, but we would be able to provide specialist advice if necessary. On the 10 July, we would have a direct line from our command cell to our post-crash management officer who was located with Silver Command. Any concerns and issues would be passed but it was our job to try to ensure that we did everything humanly possible to ensure a crash or incident would not occur in the first place. It goes without saying that an aircraft crash would be catastrophic so our focus on contingency and safety was paramount.

## Weather

Our biggest concern for the success of the flypast lay in something we had no control over – the weather.

While we had no control over it, we did have exacting weather limits laid out in our regulations to which we had to adhere. As mentioned in the opening chapter, we had to ensure that during the flypast we had a minimum of 5 kilometres of visibility at all times and that aircraft could maintain 500ft vertically clear of cloud. As such, on the day, the decision was fairly simple – it would either be good enough or not. What we hoped for was at least an overall minimum cloud-base of 1,800ft. This would enable the full flypast and egress route to be safely and legally flown. This would ensure that aircraft would at all times be 500ft clear of any ground obstructions and at least 500ft above the ground as they egressed. Over Central London, aircraft were to fly at a minimum of 1,000ft above ground level to ensure they maintained their separation distance of at least 500ft above the various tall buildings.

It wasn't just during the flypast that the weather was important. Notwithstanding the need for all aircraft to be able to see the ground as well as the aircraft ahead, we built flexibility into the holding plans to allow aircraft to hold as low as possible. Ultimately, if the weather was not fit for aircraft to descend to be able to establish themselves at 1,000ft, there was not much we could do. While we typically imagine there to be nothing to affect aircraft when operating over the sea, there often is. For the Typhoon aircraft holding off the North Norfolk coast, the rather sizeable vertical extent of the large wind farms was an issue. With some turbines being comfortably over 600ft high, not including their enormous rotating blades, the Typhoons would need to take this into account and fly slightly higher than the rest of the holding formations. Add in the sheer weight of aircraft numbers, we reasoned that we would need a minimum cloud-base of 2,000ft to safely achieve what they needed to do. For the rest of the formation hold positions, 1,500ft would be the minimum. From the holds to the ingress, the route with respect to weather was simple as these areas were flat and were within tens of feet of sea-level. This meant that as per the limits over London, we were able to apply the same criteria for the whole ingress phase. A more challenging factor was in the egress areas and routes post the Palace. In these areas, the terrain rose and we also had additional flypast locations such as Windsor Castle that were a few hundred feet in elevation higher than the Palace. These needed to be considered as the effect of this additional height, assuming the cloud-base stayed the same, would be to 'squeeze' the aircraft into a smaller gap created by the rising terrain and the cloud. If this became too small, the flight rules would be broken which removed critical safety margins. This became a real concern as the last thing we wanted was to cancel the flypast because the weather was not good enough over a secondary location but absolutely fine over London. It would make for some explaining to the public. Mitigating this absorbed a fair amount of time. Options ranged from not overflying the additional locations, having alternate routes which kept the aircraft lower in 'above sea-level' terms, or planning earlier formation 'pull up' locations such that the weather would not be a factor even if it did become worse. There was a desire to keep with the additional locations as it provided additional PR opportunities, especially for places like London Heathrow and in reality, climbing the formations out earlier was not realistic due to airspace constraints above. We resolved to handle this with careful route management and selection. We knew that each aircraft would follow an exact route and so by checking the terrain height under each of the flight-paths we could ensure that we could retain almost the same weather limits as the main event. In the end there was only a 100-ft difference in cloud-base requirements and this pertained only to the Typhoon centre-piece so, as far as we could, the issue was largely mitigated.

Despite all of the planning of the routes and attempting where possible to mitigate the effects of unfavourable weather, there was no guarantee that we would get the ideal minimum of an 1,800ft cloud-base even in July. We needed some back-up options. We generated four weather options ranging from 'Full Flypast' to Options A, B and C. In the poorest weather scenario, it would be aircraft that could travel at 140 knots or less, i.e. the helicopters and multi-engine elements of the Battle of Britain Memorial Flight. Aircraft travelling at 140 knots or less could adhere to lower weather limits and would therefore give us at least a fighting chance of a flypast. Due to the single-engine safety cases and the subsequent requirement for the Hurricane and Spitfire fighters to fly at least 150 knots, they would not be able to take part if this weather scenario was called. Just 10 knots scuppered this. Our worst-case scenario however, still needed a 1,200ft cloud-base. Providing the cloud-base was at least that, our smallest weather option looked like this:

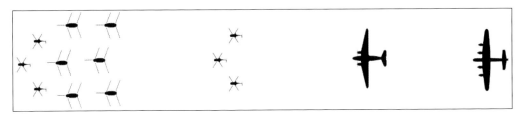

As the cloud-base improved, the subsequent weather options provided us with increasingly large formations. The next step up required an ingress cloud-base of 1,500ft and egress cloud-base of 1,600ft and would have forty-six aircraft in total. While it would still necessitate losing the iconic Typhoon centre-piece, at least it was starting to look like a sizeable formation. We wouldn't be able to put the '100' in the flypast unless we had 1,700ft on the ingress and 1,800ft on the egress. We had options all the way between these at 100ft cloud-base increments and so it would be critical on the day to obtain not only the accurate weather forecast from the Met Office, but we would also rely very heavily on the Hawk and helicopter weather-check aircraft providing us with exacting weather information. In a deteriorating weather day, making the right call could be challenging but the framework of the options versus weather limits made the task a whole lot simpler.

The remaining weather option illustrations are contained in the appendices of the book.

Although undoubtedly weather was our biggest factor and concern on the day, there were a myriad of other basic and not so basic considerations that had to be planned for, mitigated and briefed. Aircraft serviceability, illegal aircraft or drone incursion into the airspace, mid-air collision (both intra- and inter-formation), security activity including terrorist actions, medical helicopter transitions, post-flypast air-refuelling tanker requirements, loss of communications, formation leader fails to get airborne, timing contracts and sea state all needed thought.

From that list, our second most likely issue was very much internal and to an extent, also out of our control. Aircraft unserviceability could occur at any point and could happen anytime from pre-take-off, pre-hold, during the hold, post-hold, running inbound and outbound, all the way until the aircraft landed and shut-down. At each point the effect of this would be different and have a different impact on the flypast. Whereas squadrons could prepare additional aircraft to fill the gap should an aircraft fail to get airborne or turn back shortly thereafter, it became much more challenging once the aircraft had entered the hold. The holding areas were already full and each aircraft had been allocated a single 1,000ft level.

Some of the holds were adjacent to each other so the need to route aircraft clear was an additional factor. There was also not much time. Some aircraft would hold longer than others, but on average each aircraft may only be holding for around ten minutes prior to commencing their run inbound. A better option was to have additional aircraft pre-placed in the hold that would turn back if it all went to plan. We couldn't have too many due to the hold size limitations and we also did not want to wastefully leave aircraft to not participate. Not that we had much spare capacity to have the luxury to do this however. We needed to be smart with this option. While there were some Typhoons available both on the ground and as airborne spares, other back up aircraft came in the guise of additional helicopters, a C-130 Hercules and two Tornados. The two additional Tornado aircraft in particular would form an important role in trying to secure a total of 100 aircraft. For the lead up to the flypast, guarantees of having three F-35 Lightnings were slim. They had only just come over from the United States and, like all new aircraft, were having their fair share of teething problems as they settled into their new home at RAF Marham. There were also only four of them at this point and we were requesting three for the flypast. The odds of having three F-35s did not look good so if we could secure an additional two Tornado aircraft, there were options of flying a mixed formation consisting of: a single F-35 and two Tornados, or a single F-35 and one Tornado. If we had two Lightnings the additional Tornados had the option of joining the main Tornado 7-ship formation in an arrow formation similar to *Aggressor*, the Hawk T1s. A similar option was presented by the additional Hercules. We could either add it in behind the single Hercules or leave it in the hold – it would all depend on whether we managed to get 100 aircraft overall. So, while we did not have many additional options, we used our resources the best way possible and it would come down to the serviceabilities and subsequent information flow on the day as to whether we used them or not. The final decision would be made on the 10th by the SRO.

## The Known Unknowns

The flypast was a spectacle of military might and power as well as providing great photographic and PR opportunities. With this demonstration came two very real but different risks. We could provide a degree of mitigation for both, but ultimately we would need to be reactive to it. Disappointingly, ignorance and poor airmanship is a common cause of aircraft flouting the Restricted Airspace regulations. While we could put airspace in place, we could not stop someone physically flying into or through it. While it is easy to manoeuvre a single aircraft to avoid another, some of our formations were not so easy to move quickly. Aircraft incursion was a very real risk and there have been instances where this has happened. It can be catastrophic and for us the most likely place where this would occur was either in the overland ingress phase over the East of England or during the egress phase. Other than the airspace notice publication, we, through the CAA, engaged with the general aviation and gliding communities to keep them informed so that they could pass on the message to all of their pilots. Ground radar would give us a good indication should anything be untoward and Air Traffic Control were on the ball when it came to issuing messages to aircraft if they came too close via the international Guard frequency, which every aircraft should be monitoring. Within the formation, lookout and use of electronic systems such as airborne radar and TCAS (traffic collision avoidance system) could be used as well. The debate we had was whether an incursion would validate a decision to turn the formation around. In truth the principle of see (or sense) and avoid was far safer than trying to turn the whole lot around. A more worryingly trend however, was the increasing use of drones. These very small, lightweight and almost undetectable air vehicles can be flown by people with no understanding whatsoever of the airspace rules and regulations and hence their danger to aircraft. They would also be less likely to know about the routing and closure of the airspace as the flypast went overhead. Recent events on TV have highlighted the risk and disruption that unauthorised drone activity can cause, and while in theory they should not be a factor, you can't cater for everything. Flying a drone up at 1,000ft, the same height as the flypast is not difficult – albeit illegal, they are limited to 400ft currently. While often not much bigger than a bird, the impact on aircraft is far greater. Solid batteries and its structure create a far bigger hole and more damage than an equivalent weight in a bird-strike and we sought to compile reports on what sort of damage aircraft may sustain. It didn't make for comfortable reading. While we could use systems for detection, the fleeting nature of drones combined with the small size and manoeuvrability meant that on balance, trying to route the formation around it would be a challenge, if not impossible, and may still not achieve any degree of additional safety.

Some weeks in the run-up were spent discussing how the route should be publicised more generally. There was a split opinion as to whether the exact route should be made public, to increase PR opportunities, or to publicise only a very general routing. If the exact route was made public, the concern was that it could encourage increased drone or aircraft activity, which could then increase the likelihood of an airspace incursion. A document which had to go public was the airspace coordination notices and information about the Restricted Airspace. This gave a lot of information and gave the full dimensions of the airspace and times and showed the corridors where the aircraft would fly. It wouldn't be hard to work out where the aircraft would be. As the day approached, the media and public interest grew. There were requests made as to where the public could secure viewing positions outside of London as well as which other establishments, such as schools we would overfly. We had to make a compromise. We announced the general locations outside of London where the flypast could be viewed from. The towns such as Ipswich, Colchester, Witham and Chelmsford were all named in media publications. Closer in, the areas of Leyton,

Hackney and Bethnal Green were named too. We also publicised the important areas in the egress, such as Hendon, Heathrow, Runnymede and Windsor. If we encountered any drone or other airspace incursions, we would have to make the decision on the day as to how we would react depending on the severity of what we saw.

The other main risk that we considered was the outside influence of terrorist activity. While we would rely on the Security Services and police to conduct their business to negate this, we were well aware that this was a very public display with a global audience. An attack here would be broadcast instantly. While there was very little in actuality we could do other than take security updates through the day, this was one area where aborting the formation and turning them around was a real option. While fairly outlandish to consider, actions on bomb attacks through to the threat of shoulder-launched missile attacks on the aircraft were thought through. It was only the threat to the formation from shoulder-launched missiles that would most likely have prompted us to turn the formation around. Attacks on the street, including a bomb detonation would not have had an effect on the aircraft (bar a dust cloud from a bomb which aircraft could route around) so the safest thing was to continue and let the flypast go through. Of course, if any of this occurred prior to aircraft leaving the holds a decision would have been made as to whether it was prudent to continue anyway. There was always a PR perspective to consider and it was not lost on anyone that a Red Arrows flypast over a terrorist bomb attack would be most unsatisfactory.

The remaining contingencies were, to all intents and purposes, fairly standard for planning a normal military sortie – the scale was just larger. We had catered for weather in terms of cloud-base but we also needed to be aware of the sea-state. Regulations would not permit some aircraft from holding over very heavy sea conditions, typically known as sea state 6 or worse. But other than having only overland holding areas there was little we could do. If it was that poor on the day, those oversea elements would cancel – which would be the majority. We had options for aircraft unserviceability including airborne deputy and tertiary leaders should Matt and Mo in '*Windsor Lead*' go unserviceable. We had also catered for emergency helicopter activity over Central London – something which had caught us out a year earlier. While we can close the airspace, it wouldn't be justifiable to hold off an emergency ambulance helicopter which was undertaking life-saving transportation. Previous flypasts were much smaller in terms of time windows, maybe only three minutes or so, but at just under ten minutes, this represented a window of time that we needed to be able to offer safe passage for any emergency helicopter which needed to route past or through the flypast formation. Again, early engagement was key and we had procedures in place to allow medical helicopter access throughout.

While it would be highly unusual, we also needed to cater for a scenario where a formation lost visual contact with the formation ahead. With the minimum requirement of 5 kilometres visibility, this should not happen. Split by thirty seconds, all aircraft had specified times, speeds and heights to fly to. Provided they maintained this there would not be a confliction issue. Even so, the possibility of being off these constraints and then losing visual contact was there and needed to be catered for. We had already offset each formation in height, mainly in order to combat the wake turbulence that occurs behind and then slightly low of each formation. This would also provide a further degree of safety as 200ft would be between each element. The final aspect we would stipulate would require any formation which lost visual with the one in front and was off its time and speed restriction must call over the radio that it had lost visual. If this was not regained then the high formation, either ahead or behind, could 'flinch' to a higher altitude of 1,400ft. This would then put 400ft between the two formations and give us a comfortable margin of separation. The next task would be then to regain visual contact.

The final aspect to contingency planning had been to pre-position an air-refuelling tanker aircraft near to RAF Coningsby in an orbit should any of the recovering fast jet aircraft need additional fuel. We were very conscious that both Coningsby and Marham would be recovering large numbers of aircraft all around the same time. While this is no problem if all runs smoothly, we needed to consider what we would do should the first aircraft, or any other, crash on landing. The standard procedure would be to divert the aircraft to alternate airfields and each had that option, but having a fuel station in the sky also gave us an additional contingency measure should we need it. To specifically cater for the large number of Typhoons due to recover, we asked for and received the additional assistance of RAF Lakenheath to accept any diverting aircraft.

## Planning the Abort

Aside from an individual aircraft emergency which may see it exiting the formation and clearing the Restricted Airspace, nearly all of the other non-weather-related contingencies led us down one of two action scenarios. Either we would continue with the flypast and let it proceed as planned, or we would Abort and turn the whole lot around and return them back to their holding positions to await further air traffic instructions to allow them to recover back to either their planned airfield or a diversion airfield.

If the Abort option was called, the simplest scenario was that at the time of calling it, no aircraft had left their holding patterns. If this was the case, they could simply stay where they were and await further instructions. Where it all became a lot more complex was where aircraft and formations had started to leave their holds and commenced their run-in towards London. With the first formation over the Palace at 1200Z, our main Go / No-Go call would be made at 1125Z. Primarily this would be focused on making sure that the weather was sufficient, but we would also ensure that we had no security concerns at this point. Shortly after that, some of the formations would start leaving their holds. However, the planning had sought to minimise any possible conflictions to as late as possible so an Abort call up until 1140Z could be handled with relative ease. Up until 1140Z, a number of aircraft would still either be in their holds or routing inbound but not yet formed with other formations. Therefore, actioning a return back to their hold, if they had left, would be a simple affair. Post that moment however, each formation would need separate instructions as to what to do should an Abort be called. With detailed planning, it became evident that as the time progressed onwards, and as each formation left their hold, we would need to divide the Abort actions into sections depending on where, geographically, the formations were. The best way of doing this was to allocate time segments and then issue each individual formation with an Abort procedure should the call be made during that period. We also needed to be aware of the time delay between making the decision in the Command Cell, routing it to the supervisor in Swanwick Air Traffic Control and them issuing it to all of the aircraft. In addition, once the message had been received, all aircraft would need to acknowledge the Abort call and action it at the same time. To further complicate matters, the formations could be on different frequencies depending on where they were when the call was made.

Calling an Abort is therefore complex, but not necessarily complicated. What became very evident through the Abort planning process was that the call should be made only in the most extreme of circumstances as the Abort procedure would become more challenging the later it came.

The core concepts remained unchanged from the provision of safety at all times that had led the planning of the flypast. The focus remained on keeping aircraft inside the Restricted Airspace where possible, noting that turning aircraft around inside a narrow corridor would necessitate them coming very close to the edge of the corridor and potentially close to other general aviation traffic, which could legally be just outside observing. We also attempted to keep the procedure as similar as possible despite the changing time-segments. Sometimes it was possible and others not, but simplicity was key.

The following is an excerpt from the Abort plan which each aircraft would follow:

Between 1146:01 – 1154:00Z.

*Vortex* and *Spectre* are to turn right to route direct to STAPLEFORD.

*Dakota* and *Memorial* are to turn left and right respectively and return to their hold positions.

*Warboys* are to turn left and return to WATTISHAM Hold 9, *Swift* will turn right and route to WATTISHAM Hold 10.

*Snake* shall commence a left turn and return to the hold.

*Zorro* shall turn right and return to the hold, *Grizzly* shall turn left and return to the hold, *Blackcat* are to turn right and route back to their original hold.

*Snapshot* shall turn left and return to the hold, *Tartan* shall turn right and return to the hold, *Goose* shall turn left and return to the hold and *Sentry* are to turn right and return to the hold.

*Aggressor* shall turn left and return to their hold.

*Ninja* will turn right and return to the hold, *Monster* shall turn left and return to the hold.

*Gibson* will turn left and route to RAF MARHAM (note: avoid Sizewell).

*Warlord*, *Cobra* and *Triplex* will turn right, egress north and return to their respective holds.

*Red Arrows* are to turn right, head north and contact Swanwick (Mil) for climb out and onward routing.

The opposing turns which are apparent in the plan are designed to give each formation more space from that in front and behind it – again adding in safety via deconfliction.

We had these such Abort plans for: Pre-1140Z; 1140:01–1146:00Z; 1146:01–1154:00Z; 1154:01–1158:00Z; and finally, 1158:01–One Minute Prior to Formation Overhead the Palace. With the use of the mission-planning software, each of these Abort scenario time-segments were programmed in so the Abort routes each aircraft would fly could be demonstrated to everyone. We would show these in the brief and it heightened each crew's situational awareness and also proved that each Abort scenario was safe and aircraft would be deconflicted from each other.

There were, however, two particular time segments where planning the Abort was very challenging and gave us cause for concern. The first was between 1154:01–1158Z. During this time, the Typhoon '100' formation would be heading south before joining the main flypast formation from the north near Ipswich. The Typhoons would, at this stage, still be three loose formations laterally separated by around 6 miles but would need to start a right hand turn to get themselves aligned with the track inbound to London. Only once they were heading inbound would they close up to form the '100'. They would be joining behind the formations of the Tornado and F-35 and in front of the Red Arrows which would have routed in from the eastern Southwold hold areas. An abort scenario at the point just before the Typhoons would start to turn showed that a calamity would occur. With formations ahead and behind, the Typhoons would be positioning into the hole generated by these formations. If an Abort was called, the Typhoons would have nowhere to go. For safety they would all have to turn one way, either west- or east-bound, before flying north to clear the area. Whichever way they turned, it would be into a confliction with the other formation. The planning team, in conjunction with the Typhoon crews, worked on this scenario for some time to see whether other options could be generated to make a safe Abort at this point. In the end, we found no safe way of actioning an Abort for the whole formation without a confliction being generated. As the Abort had to occur for the whole flypast formation at once, we had to accept that there would be a short period of time where we would have to let the formation continue to flow towards London. No Abort would be called between 1154:01Z–1158:00Z. Based on this at the latest time of 1158Z, the leading elements, *Vortex*, would only be 3 miles from the Palace – and well within view of the TV cameras and public.

The second challenging time segment was much more flexible and would depend on the individual formation's geographic and time-based position. With the first elements overflying from 1200Z at thirty second intervals, it would make no sense for a formation to start aborting and returning back down its track if it was either over the Palace or post the Palace. But at a length of nine minutes and fifteen seconds long, we needed to retain an Abort option should circumstances dictate. With the last time segment concluding at 1158:00Z, it also meant that the formation was now fully formed in a straight line and pointing on track at the Mall and Palace. We could resume an Abort option as before. To overcome the requirement of not turning aircraft back that had already passed through we ensured that the time segment ran from 1158:01Z to each individual formation's one minute to go point. We decided that once each formation was within one minute to go – 1½ miles for the slowest movers at the front and 5 miles for the fast jet elements they would continue through and fly their pre-described egress plan.

For all of the time-segmented periods, the main difficulty faced was how to turn around twenty-two Typhoons following a decision to Abort. The time taken to turn the complete formation – safely – through 180 degrees may well be longer than it would take for the formation, which was in front, to catch up as they too turned around. We had a possible confliction and it was due to the centre '0'. The outer elements were the simplest to solve. They could turn outwards from each other with the '1' turning right and outer '0' turning left. That generated space from each other and although they were sizeable formations, they were relatively manoeuvrable in their own right. To safely gain enough separation for the centre '0', it would need to extend its track in order to clear the other Typhoon element, but in doing so would close their separation with the preceding formation. We looked at options using height and speed but these threw up other problems. If we used height for example, we would need to climb them by at least 500ft, if not ideally 1,000ft which, on an on-the-limits weather day would either put them into cloud, or at best, be at the very base of it. This was clearly not an acceptable position to plan for. There were limits as to how much speed differential we could employ, especially accelerating or slowing a formation as large as that. It too would not work in any meaningful sense. The only other option, which initially felt absolutely counter-intuitive, was to let the centre '0' flow onwards until it was clear of all other flypast traffic and only then action its manoeuvre to turn around.

With each other formation having turned around, it meant that every formation would naturally be off the centre-line of the airspace corridor leading into London.

At 5 miles wide, the corridor was designed to allow 2½ miles separation either side as a buffer from any other non-flypast traffic. Following their turn-around, if we kept the formations flying parallel to the centre-line but just inside the airspace boundary, it would create a corridor down the centre that would be clear. The centre '0' could use this. There was never a 'good' time to have to use this option, but as each formation ahead cleared through the Palace overhead, the risk reduced. An additional benefit was that as each formation passed by, the gap between the formations would be increasing due to the speed differential – it would now be working in the opposite sense and creating a larger gap, not reducing it. Air Traffic Control were well briefed on options as to when they could take control and move the final '0' around.

Once the centre '0' had turned back it could then manoeuvre clear and return back to their hold. All in all, not that simple. For many reasons, we hoped that this whole manoeuvre would not have to be actioned.

For all of the contingency options laid before us, the critical node was getting the message out to the aircraft once a decision had been made. Normally, in a large air-operation exercise the entire formation leader would manage some of these decisions based on the information they received. They would be sitting in one of the aircraft participating in the exercise and would have a set of decisions to make as various parts of the mission evolved. These weren't typically hard and much relied upon the prior planning getting it right and removing as many obstacles to mission success as possible. However, for the scale of this flypast, the national importance and the multitude of different frequencies and locations that the formations would be operating from, we would have someone more central, not sitting in an aeroplane. Matt and Mo, leading the Tornado *Monster* formation would still hold the prestigious title of being '*Windsor Lead*', but the reality was that control came from the SRO and would be routed to Air Traffic Control to pass any messages. In peacetime, we often use aircrew to sit in the airfield's air traffic control tower in times of poor weather or should an aircraft suffer an emergency. The rationale was that they could provide assistance to the controllers with respect to what may be going on in the cockpit. With some emergency situations, they may also be able to pre-empt what assistance may be required by the aircraft before the pilot even asks. This system enhances the dynamic between the air traffic controllers and the crews flying the aeroplane and allows for good knowledge sharing which is beneficial to all. A similar principle would be applied here. Squadron Leader Dunc Hewat led the Tornado Force's Standards and Evaluation Unit, and also worked within the Force Headquarters. As someone who would also be intricately aware of the plan, it seemed only sensible that he would act as the key link between the Command Cell, the Swanwick air traffic supervisor and the air traffic controllers who would be talking to the aircraft. He would locate himself at Swanwick and we would establish a direct line on the day. That way, should anything occur we would be able to speak directly with an 'aircrew man on the inside', which would act as an extra layer to avoid any confusion. It was, again, a contingency post that we hoped would not be needed.

Wrapping up all of the planning and contingency options fell into two main mass planning sessions. We held these at High Wycombe and brought all of the crews, the CAA, air traffic controllers and the SRO together to ensure that we had not missed anything and that all crews were content with how their formation had been planned and, most importantly, how they interacted with the other participants. We did not want a multitude of questions on the main flypast briefing day on 28 June when a formal planning meeting would have resolved it. There was no such thing as a stupid question and each point raised was assessed on its merits and, where appropriate, incorporated into the plan. We initially had only one mass planning day, but it was evident by the end of it that a second was needed. Despite the constant back and forth with the plans, I didn't feel comfortable that we had resolved all of the issues satisfactorily. The crews came back again about a month later for another mass planning session. By the end of this, and with some minor amendments to be made, such as a change to the Battle of Britain fighter constitution being changed to two Hurricanes and three Spitfires, we knew we were almost there. The final issue of the Operation Order, a document which captured all of the pertinent details of the flypast, was completed shortly thereafter.

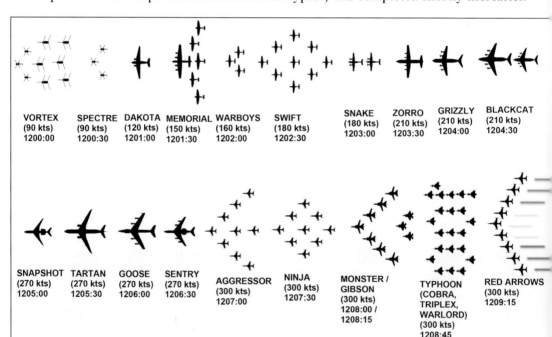

A picture paints a thousand words and this was very true in visualising the total flypast on a single page. Used as a snapshot, it provided everyone with a succinct overview of all of the participants. The additional information provided included the agreed flypast formation positions, callsign, groundspeed and time over Buckingham Palace.

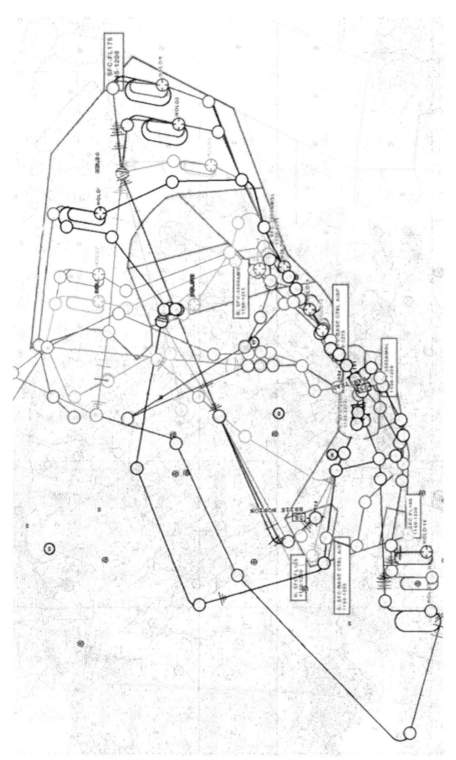

Each line represented a single formation. Each formation had between one and nine aircraft within it. Deconflicting this was a significant challenge especially after the Palace. As can be seen, a huge amount of airspace was needed to launch, hold, conduct the flypast and recovery all of the aircraft. (© Crown Copyright 2018, Wg Cdr Kevin Gatland)

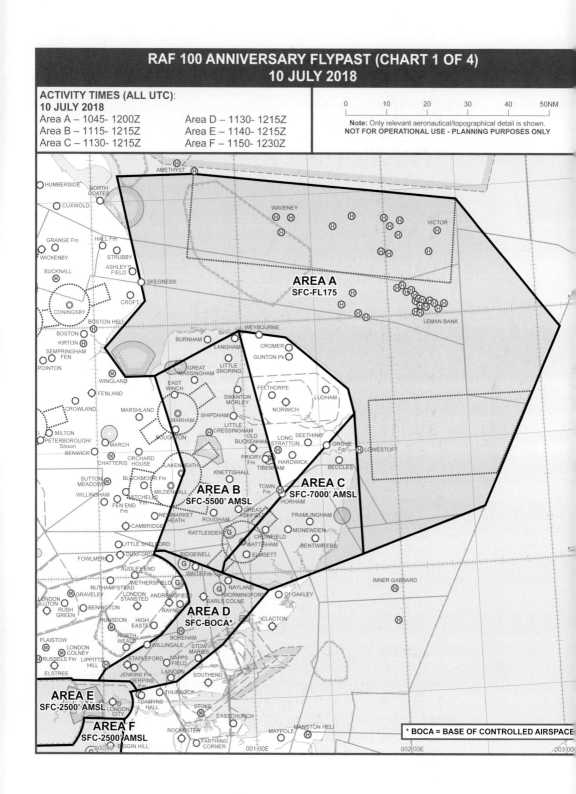

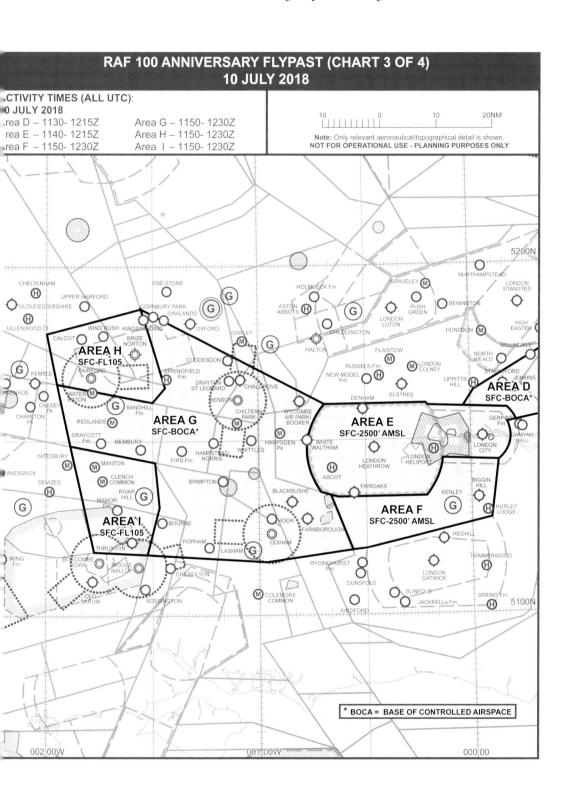

**RAF 100 ANNIVERSARY FLYPAST (CHART 3 OF 4)**
**10 JULY 2018**

CTIVITY TIMES (ALL UTC):
0 JULY 2018

| | |
|---|---|
| rea D – 1130- 1215Z | Area G – 1150- 1230Z |
| rea E – 1140- 1215Z | Area H – 1150- 1230Z |
| rea F – 1150- 1230Z | Area I – 1150- 1230Z |

10    0    10    20NM

Note: Only relevant aeronautical/topographical detail is shown.
NOT FOR OPERATIONAL USE - PLANNING PURPOSES ONLY

AREA H
SFC-FL105

AREA G
SFC-BOCA*

AREA E
SFC-2500' AMSL

AREA D
SFC-BOCA*

AREA F
SFC-2500' AMSL

AREA I
SFC-FL105

* BOCA = BASE OF CONTROLLED AIRSPACE

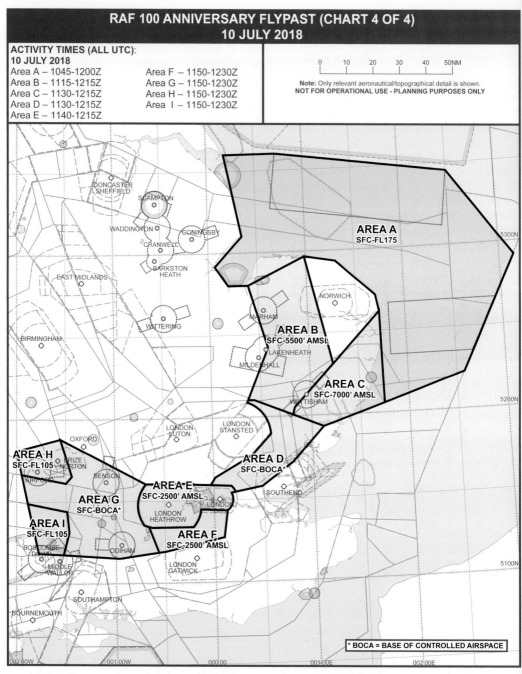

**RAF 100 ANNIVERSARY FLYPAST (CHART 4 OF 4)**
**10 JULY 2018**

ACTIVITY TIMES (ALL UTC):
10 JULY 2018

| | |
|---|---|
| Area A – 1045-1200Z | Area F – 1150-1230Z |
| Area B – 1115-1215Z | Area G – 1150-1230Z |
| Area C – 1130-1215Z | Area H – 1150-1230Z |
| Area D – 1130-1215Z | Area I – 1150-1230Z |
| Area E – 1140-1215Z | |

0    10    20    30    40    50NM

Note: Only relevant aeronautical/topographical detail is shown.
NOT FOR OPERATIONAL USE - PLANNING PURPOSES ONLY

AREA A
SFC-FL175

AREA B
SFC-5500' AMSL

AREA C
SFC-7000' AMSL

AREA D
SFC-BOCA*

AREA E
SFC-2500' AMSL

AREA F
SFC-2500' AMSL

AREA G
SFC-BOCA*

AREA H
SFC-FL105

AREA I
SFC-FL105

* BOCA = BASE OF CONTROLLED AIRSPACE

The airspace granted by the CAA was the largest ever issued. Each segment was broken into a geographic area and had specific time boundaries to minimise the disruption. While this provided a high confidence of separation between flypast and non-flypast air traffic, it could never be guaranteed and therefore posed risks we needed to consider. Non-participating aircraft would be filed against by the CAA for any infringement. (*Charts reproduced with kind permission from NATS and the CAA*)

*Chapter 6*

# RIAT Flypast Planning

Throughout much of this planning process, the possibility of putting on another flypast at the Royal International Air Tattoo (RIAT) at RAF Fairford was never far away. Although a completely different location on a different day, there were similarities and it would require the same diligent approach to airspace, deconfliction and contingency planning that was occurring for the London flypast. Just as events seem to come in threes, it was the same for this. Additionally, prior to the main London event, we would need a practice flypast which would occur over RAF Cranwell a few days before 10 July so we had been planning for that, and now there was to be an RAF 100 Flypast over the three days of RIAT, covering Friday 13 to Sunday 15 July. The marginal saving grace was that the formation would certainly be smaller than the 10th, but we didn't know at the start how much smaller. Once the idea to put on a RIAT flypast was formalised, the main challenge was capacity, both within our small planning team and then the additional workload on the flying units able to provide for these extra days. After a number of discussions with the various Force Headquarters, it was decided that we could put on a flypast in the region of fifty aircraft – i.e. half the size of 10 July, but that it should still consist of the grand centre-piece – the Typhoon '100'. It was still almost double a normal Queen's Birthday Flypast in size but felt, as we were also planning a 100-aircraft event, much more manageable. Initially, all three days were scheduled to have the same flypast arrangement, but after due consideration the fifty aircraft set-up would only be for the Friday. Some of the flying units and respective headquarters felt that their capacity to deliver the fifty-aircraft flypast over an additional three days was at very high risk. Delivering this would put a huge strain on the engineering aspects. The Saturday and Sunday were to be markedly downscaled and would therefore consist of just a Typhoon 9-ship as a tribute to the RAF 100 celebrations.

Although the airspace was much friendlier in terms of not interfering with the UK's major airports and there was clearer airspace in general around Fairford in which to operate, the Fairford flypast gave a completely new set of problems to deal with. For a start, the holding areas would not be the usual ones we had used before. Being over the other side of the country, it was simply not feasible to reuse the previous Southwold or North Norfolk coast holding areas. The aircraft wouldn't have the fuel nor the ease of transiting across the country to get to Fairford. We needed something a lot closer. Before deciding on options for the areas to hold the aircraft, the ideal track that the flypast would follow as it flew over Fairford needed to be decided. We knew that the ideal angle to view the '100' would be from head-on – just as it would be as it flew down the Mall. For Fairford we had multiple options which included it running down the length of the runway, which was east/west, or approaching from the north or the south. The spectators would all be to the south of the east-west running main runway and their viewing area therefore generally faced due north. While a left-to-right crossing or vice-versa would be manageable, it was far from the optimum approach to view the '100' in its full glory. Likewise, the flypast could have flown over the spectators from the south, but the downside to this was obvious. Many spectators would not see the flypast until it was flying away from them. This was far from ideal. This really left only one main option. The flypast needed to come in from the north and overfly the centre of the main runway heading due south. We would also need a straight line run-in of at least 10 miles and preferably more. Based on this decision, the holding areas could be examined in more detail.

Two main hold areas were looked at – one to the north of Fairford over the Wales/England border, and the other was oversea, south of Weymouth, Bournemouth and Southampton. The main driver would be minimising the impact to the civilian aviation community while ensuring ease of approach to deliver a successful flypast. The southern areas, while relatively clear of major civilian traffic, may well have had a degree of impact on the large civilian airports of Southampton and Bournemouth. The main problem, however, came in how we would fuel-efficiently manoeuvre the formation around to get them all on a final heading of south – having come from the south. This would have necessitated passing very wide and out of view of Fairford and then completed a full 180-degree turn which, as mentioned before, was problematic, especially for the Typhoon '100'. We could have changed the approach angle to a less optimum westerly or easterly heading but the impact of the spectacle of the formations would have been lost. The southern holding areas, in essence, failed in the planning analysis as they were not able to optimally deliver our requirements. With the southern areas ruled out, the only remaining feasible holding area was the northern Welsh holds.

This was still not simple. It meant holding the aircraft over the higher terrain on the Wales/England border some 30–80 miles north of Fairford. Weather once again was going to be even more a risk factor as our cloud-base requirements would be even higher than that for London. But it did solve our approach angle problem as well as minimising the disruption to civilian air traffic. Or so we thought. While planning for this continued, we did not realise at the time that the same weekend was also due to host a major national gliding competition held by the British Gliding Association (BGA). To the north of Fairford were the gliding airfields of Bidford and Long Marston. It was expected that a large number of gliders would be using these airfields as well as the surrounding airspace over the same weekend. The routing from the holds and inbound to Fairford that we had devised would mean that the airfields and airspace would not be useable for the short duration that we would need it to be active. This would have a major impact. Prior to submitting our airspace requests to the CAA, we engaged with the gliding community to see what we could negotiate. We understood their issues and looked to see whether the main flypast on the Friday could be altered. In an attempt to release airspace, the flypast routing would have to be amended quite significantly. Its impact, as well as having to alter a couple of other holding areas for non-Typhoon aircraft, was too great and we couldn't feasibly see a better option to achieve our aim. While we could not really do anything about the Friday event, our smaller Typhoon 9-ship planned for Saturday and Sunday could be rerouted to have a negligible impact on the gliding activity. Being far more manoeuvrable, turning them to change their line-up was not a problem. In addition, it mattered little whether they approached head-on or down the length of the runway. So, with this we elected for a westerly approach to Fairford. The holding area stayed the same but the route ingress went further south to try to keep as clear as possible of the gliding activity.

The egress in many respects was much simpler. Although we still had to split apart fifty aircraft, some would be recovering back into Fairford (such as the Battle of Britain Memorial Flight) and some to Brize Norton, Benson and Odiham. The large twenty-two ship Typhoon formation would need to split and climb to height before routing back across the country to RAF Coningsby. For the aircraft recovering locally, i.e. back to Fairford, Brize Norton or Odiham, it did mean that we were less concerned over the weather. We reasoned that if the weather was fit for the flypast, it would almost certainly mean that the weather was fit at their home base. Post overflight, the helicopters would split off hard left and the Memorial aircraft would split off to the right, which naturally opened up the south in order to deconflict the other aircraft. With the heavy aircraft recovering to Brize and able to remain low, and fast-jet aircraft looking to climb once they were clear of Fairford, we had a relatively simple deconflicted egress plan. It was a far cry from the complexity of London.

The key to bringing this all together was the integration of the flypast plan into the RIAT airshow schedule. My main contact here was Tom Gibbons, the Air Operations Manager for the Air Tattoo. Through him, and in collaboration with the Flying Display Director, we agreed a time overhead as well as ensuring that the participants that were due to depart and recover back into Fairford could be accommodated. In addition, we needed to ensure that the various standard holds that would be in use at Fairford were clear of any other aircraft, as we would be planning to route our aircraft straight through them. Integration of all of these aspects was critical. We had a set time overhead of 1315Z, but this would be mid-way through the airshow day. While we would run as close to the second timings as we could, the running order and timings of an air display can easily alter by some minutes. Timing for us was critical and, as per the London procedures, once aircraft had left the hold we couldn't alter their time over Fairford. From an organisational point of view, we also wanted efficiency in timing between the air display participants and the flypast. We knew on the day that close liaison would be required. We also had limited flexibility in airspace timing as well as aircraft fuel. Again, using the expertise of Rob Gratton and Matt Lee to facilitate us gaining a portion of Restricted Airspace, we had only a limited amount of time of available airspace protection. We elected at the planning stage to offer no option to delay the flypast – the main driver being that the Typhoons would have little more than 10 minutes of holding fuel available, and potentially less if the weather was poor over the eastern side of the country. While we had these few minutes of flexibility, we reasoned that it would be simpler for all concerned if we stuck to a fixed timing. This error of judgement in lack of flexibility was to return to us on the 13th.

For the small team we had to put together another flypast as large as this one was a huge undertaking. In many respects we were lucky that we could use the same principles from the London flypast and put them into practice here. The knowledge gleaned from what would work in the holding patterns, to communications set up with Air Traffic Control regarding squawks and frequencies enhanced our planning efficiency. Our understanding of what would work with the egress plan helped immeasurably, assisted of course by the simpler airspace structure in that part of the country. The same due diligence went into planning the contingency options as before, and thankfully, we had slightly fewer issues that we needed to deal with due to the location. The RIAT plan had been started later than the main London event but its conclusion needed to be on time for the June mass-briefing session. Thankfully we were ready.

*Chapter 7*

# Briefing and Practice

The first time all crews had been together to participate in this momentous flypast was at RAF Halton on 28 June 2018 – five days prior to the practice flypast which would be held at RAF Cranwell and twelve days before the main event over London. Previous flypast briefs we had been involved in had either been held at the main briefing rooms at RAF Marham or RAF High Wycombe. With the rather varied locations of all participating crews coming from around the country combined with the sheer number, it made both of these sites unsuitable. After a bit of searching, the briefing theatre at Kermode Hall, RAF Halton, was ideal. Set up like a lecture hall with rows of chairs sloping upwards and a large stage and presentation screen, it was perfect for what we required. It was also a relatively central location. A brief of this size, while never seen at Squadron level, is not an unusual event on large multi-national exercises of which most crews would have participated in at least one. The formats are fairly similar depending on the task but a clear, concise and accurate briefing is always a must. Critical in fact. If the tasks and safety elements are not completely understood by all crews and then, most importantly, actioned on the day it is not going too far to state that disaster waits in the wings. And we had a lot of information to impart. Arriving the night before, Matt, Mo, Kieran and myself managed to get all of the IT set up and ready for the following day. It would have been somewhat embarrassing – and a real challenge – to impart all that we had if the laptop and mission-planning system did not play ball. We rechecked it first thing in the morning, just to be sure. With all of the crews arriving for a start brief time of 1030, we had plenty of time available. We would also be doing some media interviews, some with the BBC, others for internal use. The brief and the crews' attention was paramount and we worked to ensure that there would be no distractions; the media had time before and after to gather what interviews and pictures they needed.

On arriving in the large lecture theatre, all crews were issued with a complete set of information pertinent to their formation and the overall flypast. Over the previous weeks, we had been using many versions of the 'mission materials' as it evolved and it was critical to ensure that everyone had the same version of the truth. Small tweaks here and there and various changes of information and data had occurred regularly, even in the days and hours leading up to the brief. Version control was critical. Crews were issued with a brand new 'comms card', the set of information that gave them all the information they would need to know about the flypast – air traffic frequencies, critical waypoint positions and timings, as well maps and the latest route data information which gave them the complete list of waypoints that we had painstakingly ensured were deconflicted from all of the other formations. Nothing would be left to chance and most of this information would be carried in the cockpit with them. Combined with the briefing, this day would provide a package of information that should be all the crews needed. This Mass Brief would be supplemented on the morning of the flypast with individual formation briefs held at their departure airfields where the formation leader would brief their own individual elements which would include their specific departure and recovery details, as well as the myriad of other aircraft-specific operational information.

The brief really was a culmination of all of the efforts over the previous eighteen months. Importantly, it was to formally brief and provide re-assurance to Air Vice Marshal Mayhew, as the Flypast SRO, that all elements of the preparation and understanding had been covered. The brief therefore needed to cover ground and air aspects as well as the overall command and control structure. Distilled into all of the elements the crews needed to know, they would all leave knowing what they had to do and how they fitted into the bigger picture. It was a lot to brief. We needed to discuss in detail all three of the planned flypasts. First up was the main event – London on 10 July, we then briefed the practice which would be held at RAF Cranwell. Only participating crews were required to stay for the third brief which was the RIAT flypast on the 13th.

The aim for the 10 July – Conduct a safe flypast over Her Majesty the Queen and the flypast at Buckingham Palace at 1200Z.

All aspects of the brief would be in-line with achieving that aim. While no one would be unsure of this aim, it is standard practice to formally declare it. Following on we reiterated the command and control aspects of the plan – where the SRO and myself would be located as well as how all of the individual elements interacted with each other. A flow chart showed how the pilots and crews would get their information (i.e. through Air Traffic Control) and in turn how Air Traffic Control would get their information. Unsurprisingly, the critical links were between the Command Cell at New Zealand House and the liaison officer based at Swanwick as well as between Air Traffic Control and the aircraft.

Flight safety, rules and regulations were briefed next. These were only relevant to the flypast and there were a host of other individual rules that would underpin all aspects of operating aircraft. Most were standard operating procedures but the pertinent ones were briefed. Most of these were built into the plan as we had progressed so had come as no surprise. Following the next set of slides which briefed the overall constitution, along with formation positions, heights, speeds and timings, we entered the bulk of the brief starting with a flypast overview.

This section was where the bulk of the plan started coming together. All thirteen hold locations were briefed in detail. This included who was to enter which hold, how, at what height and to which air traffic frequency they would be expecting to talk. The entry into and exit from the hold were particularly important. We would not want aircraft conflicting with aircraft already established in the hold, nor would we want them causing issues when leaving. The direction given on how to exit was clear and concise. They had to exit with awareness on the element ahead or within plus or minus five seconds and on the right speed. The formations had to exit in formation shape and could only commence a descent (if needed) once they were past a specific point. Any 'whip' aircraft also had a particular geographic point where they would leave the main formation and return to their base.

Once the formations were headed inbound, the features that they would see were shown. A few weeks previously, we had flown in an A-109 helicopter following the exact flypast route over Central London, for two reasons. The first was to confirm that the ever-developing London skyline had not put up a tall building in the vicinity which would cause us an issue (this included large cranes – which we would monitor throughout) and the second to gain up-to-date pictures of the run-in at 1,000ft so all crews would have a pictorial reference in mind prior to

Typical of the London skyline as the formation would approach Buckingham Palace. It was critical that we checked the approaches down the flypast to see whether there would be any issues such as cranes. We used the 32(R) Squadron Royal Flight Agusta A-109 for this task. (© *Crown Copyright 2018, Wg Cdr Kevin Gatland*)

conducting the flypast. Fairlop reservoir, the Velodrome and the distinctive bend in the Thames with the Waterloo and Westminster bridges, close to the Mall, were excellent visual features.

Following overflight, the egress phase was carefully briefed. It detailed each individual formation's route, speed, height and air traffic frequency to switch to. Nothing was left to chance and we had exact routes for each element. There had been some subtle changes in the final few weeks leading up to the brief; we had removed the egress holds for the Typhoons prior to crossing the airways back to Coningsby but retained the three heavy holds over Salisbury Plain.

Finally, the detail of all of the contingencies was briefed. This included all of the weather options and who would participate depending on any particular cloud-base structure, as well as expected actions on all of the elements mentioned in the previous chapter – bird-strikes, high sea state, no radio procedures, drone activity, aircraft incursion, security and/or terrorist activity, loss of aircraft or formation members, procedures for being late etc. Finally, the Abort procedure was briefed against the time segments previously mentioned.

All in all it took just under two hours to cover everything we needed and we still had two more briefs to go.

The briefing room at RAF Halton. The brief started with a time hack and Roll Call to ensure everyone who needed to be present was indeed there. (© *Crown Copyright 2018, Christopher Yarrow*)

The author opening the briefing day. For many this was the first time that the entire package of the RAF 100 formations had been seen together. (© *Crown Copyright 2018, Christopher Yarrow*)

As airborne formation leaders, a large part of the briefing fell to two outstanding aviators – Sqn Ldr Matt Axcell and Sqn Ldr Mo Abdallah. Flying the lead *Monster* aircraft, they held the prestigious callsign of '*Windsor Lead*'. (© *Crown Copyright 2018, Christopher Yarrow*)

(© *Crown Copyright 2018, Christopher Yarrow*)

There was a huge amount of information to take in. Success hinged on a well-delivered and clearly understood brief. (© *Crown Copyright 2018, Christopher Yarrow*)

(© *Crown Copyright 2018, Christopher Yarrow*)

Each formation had a bespoke flying suit patch to be worn. The full list is displayed at the end of the book. (© *Crown Copyright 2018, Christopher Yarrow*)

The RAF 100 Flypast Senior Responsible Officer, Air Vice-Marshal Gerry Mayhew summing up the briefing prior to the crews returning back to their respective bases and squadrons. It would be him, as the SRO, who would ultimately give the Go/NoGo decision on the day. (© *Crown Copyright 2018, Christopher Yarrow*)

## The Practice Flypast Events

There were a few elements that constituted the practice events that led up to the RAF 100 Flypast. We had requested that if crews were scheduled to fly in the Flypast, they should also fly in the Queen's Birthday Flypast in the previous June if possible; this would help with a greater understanding of the procedures involved. Of course there were some similarities and we had tried to cross-fertilise as many ideas as possible across both of the events.

Some of the larger formations had practised their individual elements from their home bases e.g. a Hawk diamond 9 or the helicopter formations. Indeed, we had seen evidence of this through social media. Twitter showed us the first helicopter practice images in the weeks prior with various half formations. These were fine and demonstrated to us the degree of interest that would be around on the day. The one formation that we all had agreed to keep secret was the Typhoon centre-piece. The twenty-two-ship Typhoon '100' was to be kept under wraps until the day. This was to prove a great challenge and it felt almost like a cat-and-mouse game against the many media outlets and enthusiasts that would be snapping up photos and speaking to the crews in the lead up to the event.

In the three weeks prior to 10 July, eight Typhoons and their pilots made their way down to RAF Coningsby. This would bolster the numbers being provided by the Coningsby squadrons and also split the load between the two bases. The work put in by Mike Childs and his team would now be transferred into the airborne environment. The early stage practices were to prove the initial set-up of the formation references. In one practice, a full single '0' was formed along with single aircraft representing the leads of the external '1' and '0. A further practice consisted of nine aircraft, with just the lead three aircraft in each element. These practices would allow for the confirmation of spacing, as well as give an indication of ease of manoeuvrability. We still, however, had to find a way of conducting a practice without giving the game away and being photographed as a complete '100'. Once again Twitter was the first to show us pictures of what the initial '0' and single outrigger aircraft looked like. We didn't want that happening again prior to the 10 July!

The decision was made that the main formation practices would happen over the North Sea, far from prying camera lenses and other aircraft. There was the possibility of being photographed from an oil rig or ship but it was remote and this option gave us the best possibility of remaining unseen while achieving the practice aim. The Typhoon simulator was also used to test the recovery phase and ensure that the

*(© Crown Copyright 2018, Sgt Paul Oldfield)*

The view from the rear-seat of a Typhoon inside the heart of the RAF 100 formation. This picture was taken on 27 June 2018 during one of the practice events over the North Sea. The prime reason to hold the practices over the sea were to attempt to preserve the surprise element of the iconic '100' formation. (© *Crown Copyright 2018, Wg Cdr Kevin Gatland*)

whole sortie profile worked. There were limitations as to what could be achieved in the simulator but as a proof of concept it worked well. The important stages were yet to come – getting it airborne.

On 27 June, the first full Typhoon practice occurred, and I had the opportunity to fly within the formation. It was a perfect day for it. Blue skies and barely a cloud in sight. Warm and sunny; I remarked to Tris, my pilot for the day, that I hoped that the 10 July would be as kind. It would certainly make the whole event easier and far less stressful. I had never flown in a Typhoon before and getting in was an exceptional feeling. Watching over twenty-two aircraft being crewed into at the same time was something rarely witnessed and it was certainly the largest formation of Typhoons ever to be seen thus far. As per the mass brief earlier, we taxied on time and held towards the end of the runway as we awaited our slot for departure. The message had obviously got out to the enthusiast community as there were large numbers of people poised with their cameras to get some great photos. Rolling onto the runway, the throttles were selected to maximum dry power and we accelerated down the runway. It was far faster than the Tornado which I had been used to, and this was only about half the power available – there was still the reheat take-off option. Once up, we settled into the stream of aircraft before aligning ourselves with the rest of our formation. I had the privilege of being positioned in the centre '0', mid-way down the right-hand side. I would get a great view of all of the aircraft which surrounded me. Sophie Raworth, the news correspondent from the BBC, was in the aircraft adjacent to my left. Our route took us over the North Sea and up to a few thousand feet. There was slight cloud cover below,

which I thought was a good thing. It may make getting any pictures more challenging. As each of the elements slowly closed into position, the spectacle was incredible from within the cockpit. The mass of aircraft surrounding me was something I shall never forget. Being a fair-weather day, the recovery back into Coningsby proved to be simple and straightforward – again I hoped that the weather on the 10th would be as perfect as it had been today. The debrief afterwards showed that a few reference changes would need to be made. A picture taken showed a flaw in the line astern references, which in turn meant pilots flew wide on their echelon positions. This had the effect of making

After each sortie, the formations were debriefed. Errors in execution and subsequent amendments ensured that the formation would look its best on the day. In these sets of photographs, evident spacing errors are apparent which were subsequently ironed out through the debriefing process. (© *Crown Copyright 2018*)

The final over-sea practice had it nailed. (© *Crown Copyright 2018*)

the lead aircraft in each of the three individual formations appear too long of the rest of the formation. A correction to these references was made and further practises over the days ahead proved that this flaw had been resolved. Airborne, the '100' now looked spot on.

Notwithstanding the individual element practices, and as per standard practice for the Queen's Birthday Flypast, we absolutely had to have a representative Practice Flypast to ensure not only the plan worked, but also to give the crews a chance to hone their skills in the flypast environment. It would give us an opportunity to review any niggles in the holding plan and, as best we could, the egress plan to enable any last-minute changes to be made. The day would also give the SRO and myself a perfect view of how the formations actually looked from the ground. The practice formed part of the assurance process to demonstrate that the flypast plan and constitution was safe and professional and allowed the SRO, on behalf of the Chief of the Air Staff, to give the green light to proceed to the main event on the 10th. While scheduled for 3 July, many of the formations had been practicing their individual elements in the weeks previous. We could not, of course, conduct the practice event over London, so the main practice event following the briefing day would be held overhead RAF Cranwell in Lincolnshire.

RAF Cranwell is the spiritual home of the Royal Air Force. Its history dates back to November 1915, initially as a Royal Naval Air Service training establishment but from April 1918 becoming part of the fledgling new Service called the Royal Air Force. It became known as RAF Cranwell. Its iconic feature, and one that can be seen from miles around, is the famous College Hall Officers' Mess building. Built between 1929 and 1933, it sits to the north of the main road which separates the main airfield to the south. It is one of the few RAF bases that you can literally drive straight through the middle of. Today the base trains all RAF Officers through Initial Officer Training. Every officer participating in the flypast would, some years earlier, have passed through Cranwell and would know the base and area very well.

In terms of a practice location, Cranwell is very well suited but it would mean crafting a bespoke plan in as much detail as has been discussed over the previous chapters. One major benefit in conducting the practice at Cranwell was that the airspace around it was so much more permissive, far less dense in terms of aircraft movements and comfortably away from any major airports. As before, we would need a complete holding plan, ingress route, egress route and recovery planned. We would also need a new Restricted Airspace plan to be agreed as well as Air Traffic Control frequencies and squawks. True enough, there were some aspects of the London plan we could utilise – the distances in use were similar so we could use the same holds and a small part of the initial exit plan from the hold, but it was really there that the similarities ended. Once the aircraft left their holds, the routes would need to swing northwards rather than head south and south-west towards London. This wasn't too much of a problem for all of those aircraft holding in the Southwold holds, but it meant significant changes needed to be made for all of those holding in the North Norfolk coast holds as they would not be travelling as far south as for the main event. The meshing of all of the aircraft routes would also need to be completed in the vicinity of RAF Marham in order to align the aircraft on the right track.

The egress of the whole formation was our most challenging phase and we did not want to waste the opportunity to practice it where we could. One of the stipulations which we placed on our planning was that where we could, the egress routing should replicate as closely as possible the actual egress procedures. This meant that we would fly the same heading changes, same speeds and same distances to simulate what we would be doing over London a week later. These were made accurate to the degree in heading and knot in speed. This was important as it would allow all of the crews to fly either exactly as, or as close as possible to, the plan for the 10th. The practice event needed to demonstrate that the whole concept worked, not just that the aircraft looked good in their formations as they passed the clocktower at Cranwell. This was particularly pertinent to those flying in the large formations. The practice that they

The first formation – callsign *Vortex* arriving at RAF Cranwell leading the practice event. (© *Crown Copyright 2018, Gordon Elias*)

would get manoeuvring the formation around with the same heading changes and distances to run would be invaluable and would allow us to make any minor (and hopefully no major) changes to the plan.

There were a number of other planning amendments which had to be made which would differ from the main event. The helicopter formations would forward deploy to RAF Wittering to assist with their fuel plan, and the paucity of available flying hours on the Battle of Britain Memorial Flight aircraft meant that they would be simulated by a single Tutor, for the DC-3, and Tucano, for the remaining Lancaster and fighter aircraft. Similarly, the Red Arrows would not participate in the practice, but as they were at the back of the stream as the final formation, it did not create any issues.

As all of the planning for this separate flypast occurred it was, of course, in conjunction with planning the main event, and RIAT. The team were busy. It was a relief to get to the day itself. Mother Nature had smiled on us and we had a day of fantastic weather. On arriving at Cranwell we set in process the same command and control procedures we planned to use in London on the 10th. It was slightly more difficult however, because prior to the flypast a large media facility had been set up which saw us balancing the

*Vortex* cross the parade square in front of where I first joined the RAF – No 1 Mess. The RAF College Hall 'Orange' can be seen at the bottom of the picture. (© *Crown Copyright 2018, Gordon Elias*)

*Spectre*, made up of Juno and Jupiter aircraft were next. (© *Crown Copyright 2018, Gordon Elias*)

The formation of nine Tucano from RAF Linton-on-Ouse made up *Swift* formation. (© *Crown Copyright 2018, Gordon Elias*)

Two Shadow aircraft from 14 Squadron. The Shadow R Mk 1 is a modified Beechcraft King Air 350 series aircraft operating in the intelligence, surveillance and reconnaissance role from RAF Waddington. (© *Crown Copyright 2018, Gordon Elias*)

Two Hercules C-130 aircraft callsign *Zorro*. The practice gave us an opportunity to fly both C-130 aircraft in formation – a back-up plan for the main event. As it turned out, both participated so it was a practice well worth having. (© *Crown Copyright 2018, Gordon Elias*)

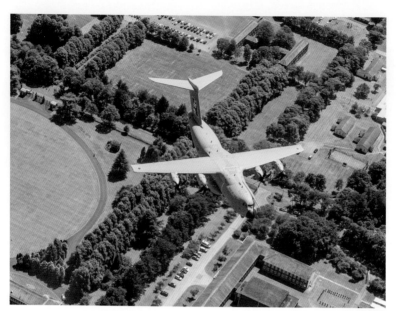

The Atlas followed the Hercules aircraft. The type was the latest to join RAF service arriving in November 2014 at RAF Brize Norton. (© *Crown Copyright 2018, Gordon Elias*)

A mixed formation of a C17 Globemaster and a Royal Flight BAe 146. Callsign *Blackcat*, the C17 was operated by 99 Squadron and the BAe 146 operated by 32 Squadron. 2018 was also 99 Squadron's centenary year as well. (© *Crown Copyright 2018, Gordon Elias*)

The Hawk T2 are operated by IV Squadron at RAF Valley. The latest generation fast-jet training aircraft in the RAF, the squadron teaches air-air as well as air-ground tactics prior to pilots leaving for conversion training on the Typhoon or F-35 Lightning. (© *Crown Copyright 2018, Gordon Elias*)

Tornado GR4. Callsign *Monster*. *Monster 1* was also the formation lead for the day and was flown by Squadron Leader Matt Axcell and Squadron Leader Mo Abdallah. The type was to retire in March 2019 following over four decades of service. (© *Crown Copyright 2018, Gordon Elias*)

*Gibson* formation was a single F-35 Lightning flanked by two Tornado GR4. This formation was one of the back-up options should we not have the requisite three F-35s available on 10 July. (© *Crown Copyright 2018, Gordon Elias*)

Only the leading elements of the Typhoon '100' were to participate on the practice. The remainder of the practice events were held over the North Sea to ensure secrecy and surprise! (© *Crown Copyright 2018, Gordon Elias*)

Superb view from above the leading edges of the Typhoon formation on the practice event (© *Crown Copyright 2018, SAC Wade*)

For the main practice event at RAF Cranwell, we only utilised the leading edges of the Typhoon formation. The view from the cockpit here is shown from the furthest outside aircraft forming the '1'. (© *Crown Copyright 2018, SAC Wade*)

flypast control actions with the requests from the media for information and interviews about the flypast. We did manage to keep them largely separate and had the majority of the media event after the aircraft had flown over and departed.

Overall, the practice day had proved a complete success. There were some minor aspects that we needed to tighten up and resolve, but all in all the plan had worked. We had always been very tentative about whether the F-35s would make an appearance. They had arrived in the UK earlier but had only been present for a few weeks. They were still very small in number and had their own teething problems to resolve. Nevertheless, we managed to get one of the three F-35s into the practice. In some respects this proved to be advantageous as it allowed us to fly a contingency option where we used the two spare Tornado aircraft to fly in formation. We also managed to fly the additional C-130 to make a pair.

Our next event was the day itself. Nervously we watched the weather and awaited the 10 July.

## Chapter 8

# The Main Event – 10 July 2018

## New Zealand House

It was a euphoric feeling. But counting down the minutes as 1200Z approached felt agonising. I could not see the formations yet but I knew that all of the hard work from the team would be coming to fruition very shortly. Once the first formation went over the Palace, there would only be a further nine minutes and fifteen seconds of the spectacle. I saw the last Heathrow-bound commercial aircraft overhead for a while; departures and recoveries would be held for the duration of the flypast. I waited eagerly, apprehensively and with a sense of wonder as I saw Trafalgar Square come to a halt. Everyone seemed to be outside. Rooftops were massing people, the bridges in the distance seemed full. We could hear the throng of the Mall. The three helicopters appeared in position ready to film from the air as well as take some of the most outstanding photographs. About ten minutes prior, people started flooding out of the buildings to watch; the BBC coverage still continued in the background on our iPad.

And then…. A slight glimmer of lights in the distance. *Vortex*, our lead formation of three Pumas and six Chinooks, glistened into view. We couldn't hear them yet, but here they were. It was about to start.

## Airborne – a pilot's perspective

Tornado GR4 of *Monster* formation getting airborne to participate in the flypast. Only one aircraft of each fleet was adorned with the RAF100 tail design. (© *Crown Copyright 2018, Sgt Nik Howe*)

Having only recently arrived in the UK from the US, the fifth generation F-35B Lightning gets airborne from RAF Marham. It was only in the final stages that its participation was confirmed. (© *Crown Copyright 2018, Sgt Nik Howe*)

(© *Crown Copyright 2018, Steve Lympany*)

(© *Crown Copyright 2018, Steve Lympany*)

Voyager KC Mk 2 – the largest aircraft in the flypast. (© *Crown Copyright 2018, Steve Lympany*)

(© *Crown Copyright 2018, Steve Lympany*)

The Atlas C Mk 1 callsign *Grizzly* takes off from RAF Brize Norton. (© *Crown Copyright 2018, Steve Lympany*)

(© *Crown Copyright 2018, Steve Lympany*)

The venerable Hercules. A true workhorse, not only for the RAF but for air forces around the world. Tremendously capable and a real sight if seen flying in the low-level environment through the valleys and hills of the UK. (© *Crown Copyright 2018, Steve Lympany*)

Another workhorse of the RAF – the C17 Globemaster. We initially wanted larger numbers of these heavy aircraft to participate in the flypast but availability was a challenge. (© *Crown Copyright 2018, Steve Lympany*)

(© *Crown Copyright 2018, Steve Lympany*)

Flown by 32 (The Royal) Squadron, the BAe 146 provides VIP transport for the Royal Family as well as senior politicians and other dignitaries. (© *Crown Copyright 2018, Steve Lympany*)

(© *Crown Copyright 2018, SAC James Skerrett*)

Typhoon numbers on show! RAF Coningsby became the Typhoon RAF 100 Flypast hub with aircrew, groundcrew and aircraft deployed down from RAF Lossiemouth to support. All of this required tremendous coordination in both the engineering and aircrew domains. (© *Crown Copyright 2018, Cpl Steve Buckley*)

We had planned, briefed and were ready. The Command Cell located in London had given us the go. We were inbound. It's very odd flying over Central London. We normally spend our time avoiding towns and cities – or flying very high over them. But at 1,000ft, and at speeds that allow you to see things, it is a remarkable feeling. The lower than normal height makes it feel almost a bit surreal. Should we really be here?

The features that had been briefed two weeks earlier when we had all got together at RAF Halton started coming into view. We had left the holding pattern on time and on height. We were in good shape. From coasting in, passing the old airfield at Bentwaters and clipping the large towns of Ipswich, Colchester and Chelmsford, the lake at Fairlop is the first main feature that lines you up with the Mall – we are still about 11 miles away at this point; the Mall cannot be seen but you know you are on track.

We changed to the Flypast Primary frequency. The headings and timings are checked again, an aircraft systems check is completed by the crew to ensure everything is working as expected. It is. The green and yellow fields start becoming fewer and the conurbations start building more and more. In the distance, glimpses of large skyscrapers become apparent. London is looming. The visibility is better than the pictures we had seen at the brief. One minute, fifteen seconds to go. Directly ahead is

*Vortex* in formation tracking towards London. (© *Crown Copyright 2018*)

An outstanding view from the rear of the Chinook formations *Vortex* as they manoeuvre into position prior to London. (© *Crown Copyright 2018, SAC Amy Lupton*)

(© *Crown Copyright 2018, Cpl Steve Buckley*)

(© Crown Copyright 2018, Cpl Steve Buckley)

(© *Crown Copyright 2018, Cpl Steve Buckley*)

(© *Crown Copyright 2018, Cpl Steve Buckley*)

After exiting their respective holds off the North Norfolk coast, all three Typhoon formations made their way south-bound overland over East Anglia to join together. Only towards the latter stages did they finally join together closely to resemble the '100'. A 'whip' aircraft circled above to ensure all aircraft were correctly in position before it departed leaving the main formation to stick together tightly as they approached London. (© *Crown Copyright 2018, Cpl Steve Buckley*)

Fairlop reservoir was one of the first line-up features that the crews would use as they approached London. This photo was taken by the author during the recce sortie from the Agusta A-109. (© *Crown Copyright 2018, Wg Cdr Kevin Gatland*)

With the canard of the 'whip' Typhoon in view as the pilot circled overhead the main formation to ensure that they all looked perfect, his role was critical in making any last-minute corrections on the run in. This Typhoon would depart just prior to the main formation entering London airspace. (© *Crown Copyright 2018, Cpl Steve Buckley*)

Now fully formed, the Typhoon '100' is routing inbound to Buckingham Palace. (© *Crown Copyright 2018, Cpl Steve Buckley*)

The 'Pringle' is now in view. Although we had great visibility on the day, murky conditions can make these distinctive features challenging to see. (© *Crown Copyright 2018, Wg Cdr Kevin Gatland*)

(© *Crown Copyright 2018, SAC Rose Buchanan*)

the 'Pringle' – or more formally the Lee Valley VeloPark. Built in 2011 and used for the 2012 Olympics, we pass down its left-hand edge – its distinctive shape shows we remain on track. Timing is critical, we are working to plus or minus five seconds and with aircraft ahead and behind, we cannot afford to be off this timeline.

We can see the aircraft ahead, slightly high. This gives confidence that we are on the right track too. Passing the Pringle, the next feature to look for is the distinctive curve in the Thames. This key feature leads our eyes onto the Mall. We do have very accurate navigation systems such as GPS of course, but nothing beats the confidence of seeing the features you know need to be seen. Everything is hand-flown, despite the automation most aircraft have nowadays, the hands are on both throttle and stick. We are glad for the weather; the visibility makes it easy to see the aircraft in front and no cloud near makes for a much easier flypast. I think briefly about the egress – from the reports the weather is good there too. That removes a huge amount of complication. It gets bumpier – it's always bumpy over London – it must be something to do with the amount of concrete, buildings and reflected heat. It makes formation flying more difficult but the pilots either side of us hang on in there. The formation must look

The view of Spitfire XVI, TE311 from the rear turret of the Battle of Britain Memorial Flight Lancaster PA474. This Lancaster is just one of two airworthy aircraft from the 7,377 that were built. (© *Crown Copyright 2018, SAC James Skerrett*)

tight. The curve of the Thames, the two bridges lead our eyes to the right. The Mall comes into view. Drawing my eyes up, Buckingham Palace is also now in sight. We are nearly there. Forty-five seconds to go. I can see the media and police helicopters above and clear of our formation. A slight nudge on the throttle ensures we stick glued on our timeline. The aircraft ahead passes over the Palace and starts its egress manoeuvre. We will follow thirty seconds later. The Mall is packed, there must be thousands of people watching. It really is a true spectacle and I hope that it looks as spectacular from the ground. Flying over the Mall we are heading directly towards the Palace but slightly offset – the wind effect at height often means that our heading and actual track line over the ground are different. We fly over-top. On time. The planned extension of 0.6 miles post the Palace allows for the aircraft not to start an immediate turn as soon as we hit the overhead – it looks much better for the spectators. The job is not yet complete, we are now into the egress phase.

The final view as Buckingham Palace is approached. It can be seen just off-centre of the left main windscreen. (© *Crown Copyright 2018, SAC Kitty Barrett*)

The Royal Family on the balcony watching the RAF 100 Flypast. (© *Crown Copyright 2018, SAC Chris Thompson-Watts*)

(© *Crown Copyright 2018*)

*Vortex* – the first formation overhead. Now into the egress phase. (© *Crown Copyright 2018, SAC Pippa Fowles*)

The clearly marked final approach to the Palace is evident with this outstanding view down the Mall. The key was to line up the formation as best you could down the centre of the Mall to fly directly over the Palace. (© *Crown Copyright 2018, SAC Amy Lupton*)

(© *Crown Copyright 2018, SAC Pippa Fowles*)

*Vortex*, the first formation flies overhead the Palace at exactly 1300 hrs, marking the start of the iconic flypast. (© *Crown Copyright 2018, WO Andy Malthouse*)

This overhead shot of *Dakota*, the second formation in the flypast, shows the incredible turnout down the Mall. (© *Crown Copyright 2018, Cpl Tim Laurence*)

(© *Crown Copyright 2018, Cpl Tim Laurence*)

The third formation, *Memorial*. Historic and recognised the world over are the Lancaster, Spitfire and Hurricane aircraft of the Second World War era. (© *Crown Copyright 2018*)

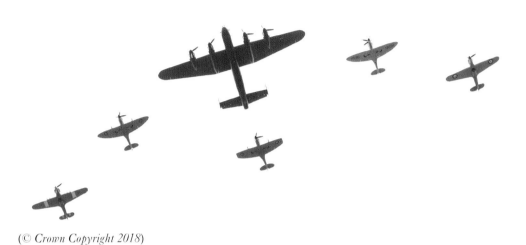

(© *Crown Copyright 2018*)

*Swift* – the formation of nine Tucano aircraft. (*Mr Andy Chase*)

Following *Swift*, were two Shadow aircraft in formation with callsign *Snake*. (© *Crown Copyright 2018*)

A superb cockpit shot from inside the second Hercules. Callsign *Zorro 2*, the second Hercules was a planned contingency option which was used on the day. (© *Crown Copyright 2018, Mr Paul Crouch*)

*Zorro*. The two Hercules in formation as they pass down the Mall and over the Palace. (© *Crown Copyright 2018*)

The Atlas over the Victoria Monument. Callsign *Grizzly*, we had initially hoped for four of these magnificent aircraft to participate in the flypast. (© Copyright 2018 Sgt Tim Laurence.)

The incredible view down the Mall. (© *Crown Copyright 2018*)

An unusual formation of the C17 Globemaster leading the BAe 146 from The Royal Flight. Callsign *Blackcat*, these aircraft are normally based at RAF Brize Norton and RAF Northolt respectively. (© *Crown Copyright 2018, Cpl Tim Laurence*)

(*Mr Andy Chase*)

The Voyager, callsign *Tartan*, the largest aircraft in the Royal Air Force's inventory flies towards the Palace. We managed to get 100 passengers on board to witness and enjoy this spectacular event from a very different vantage point. Normally used to medium and high-level operations, flying at this height over Central London gave the passengers a once-in-a-lifetime experience. (© *Crown Copyright 2018, Cpl Tim Laurence*)

A recent addition to the RAF's inventory was the RC-135W Rivet Joint. Callsign *Goose*, this aircraft was based at RAF Waddington and flown by 51 Squadron. It normally performs electrical surveillance soaking up electronic emissions from communications, radar and other systems. (© *Crown Copyright 2018, Cpl Tim Laurence*)

The final 'heavy' aircraft was the E–3D Sentry. Operating as an Airborne Warning and Control system, the giant dish on the aircraft spine provides a very distinctive recognition feature and is considered a high value asset to be protected in any air war. *Sentry* is flown by 8 Squadron. (© *Crown Copyright 2018*)

The start of the fast-jet formations was led by 100 Squadron, callsign *Aggressor*. Normally based from RAF Leeming, the Hawks deployed to RAF Wittering and recovered to RAF Boscombe Down in order to ensure the fuel plan worked. (© *Crown Copyright 2018*)

The second fast-jet formation to pass over the Palace was *Ninja*. This generation of Hawk aircraft was based at RAF Valley and provides fast-jet flying training to pilots prior to them commencing their front-line conversion unit training. (*Mr Andy Chase*)

The final two Tornado GR4 squadrons, No IX and No 31 Squadron flew together in the flypast. What is unfortunately not seen in this picture, is the additional two aircraft in trail taking the total GR4 participation to nine. The type disbanded in March 2019 after four decades of service and formed the backbone of strike / attack capability of the RAF until the very end. The author amassed some 2200 hrs in this type. Their callsign on the day was

After much debate about whether the F–35B Lightning would make it into the flypast, we managed to secure three. At the time of the flypast, there were only four aircraft in the UK. Flown by 617 Squadron under the callsign *Gibson*, a callsign in memory of Wing Commander Guy Gibson who led the Dams raids during the Second World War, the aircraft are cutting-edge fifth generation air systems. (© *Crown Copyright 2018, Cpl Tim Laurence*)

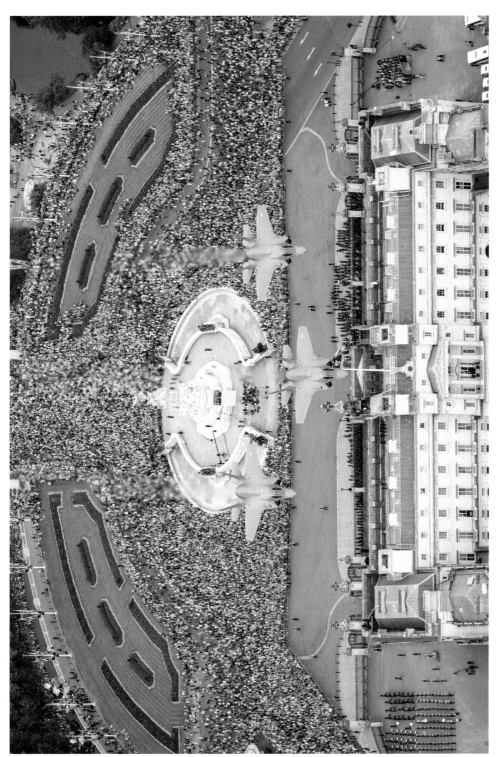

(© *Crown Copyright 2018. WO Andy Malthouse*)

An incredible set of pictures displaying the twenty-two Typhoon aircraft in the '100' formation. From where we were positioned at New Zealand House in the Command Cell, the atmosphere from the crowd when the formation came into view was palpable. I doubt anyone will forget the incredible noise of twenty-two EJ200 engines powering the Typhoons down the Mall. Simply outstanding work. (© *Crown Copyright 2018, Cpl Tim Laurence*)

The finale of the RAF100 Flypast was left to the iconic Red Arrows. Sporting their distinctive red Hawk T Mk 1 aircraft, the Reds never fail to disappoint and were loved by the public watching the display. (© *Crown Copyright 2018, Cpl Tim Laurence*)

(© *Crown Copyright 2018, Cpl Helen Rimmer*)

(© *Crown Copyright 2018, SAC Sarah Gregory*)

(© *Crown Copyright 2018, SAC Rose Buchanan*)

(*© Crown Copyright 2018*)

## On the Dias with the Chief of the Air Staff

About a week or so prior, it had struck me that on current plans, CASWO (Chief of the Air Staff's Warrant Officer) and I were not going to see any of the flypast. We would be on the Dais, facing the Balcony of Buckingham Palace, waiting for the Queen and the Royal Family to emerge. As they did, we would both salute, and remain facing Her Majesty during the flypast, as protocol demanded that she should not see us with our backs turned. So the flypast would arrive up the Mall behind us, and there would be no gap between the peak of our caps and the Palace for us to see as it passed overhead. I did not want to miss this spectacular flypast, and I did not want in all subsequent conversations about the flypast to have to say, 'I've heard it was good, but I didn't see any of it at the time.' So, on the basis that Her Majesty would be looking at the flypast and not down at us, I asked the Ceremonial team to propose to the Palace that we would face the Queen until we saw her head go up to look at the start of the flypast; then we would about-turn to face down the Mall; and then when the Red Arrows approached at the end of the flypast, we would about turn and face Her Majesty again. That went through on the nod, which allowed CASWO and me to enjoy one of the finest possible views of the flypast. I had said to him in advance that we needed to be careful not to speak to each other when we were together on the Dais, especially when we were facing down the Mall, with a whole battery of cameras on the Victoria Monument opposite us, ready to pick up on whatever we were saying. It was I who broke our discipline: as the '100' of Typhoons came into view, and I could hear a wave of cheering noise rolling towards us from the tens of thousands on the Mall, through pursed lips I said 'CASWO, I'm starting to get a bit emotional here', and in a choked voice he replied, 'Me too, sir'. It was a touching moment in itself, and I was glad to have someone that I could share my thoughts with at this historic, never to be repeated moment.

# RAF Fairford – 13 July 2018

While the London flypast on 10 July went without a hitch, that could not be said for its sister flypast which was planned for Friday 13 July at Fairford. Having briefed the crews previously at Halton and toting fifty aircraft, it was the Centenary celebration flypast for the RAF at the Royal International Air Tattoo and was to be a real highlight for the crowds assembled there. The initial weather picture first thing in the morning showed a main cloud-base of around 3,500–4,000ft with good visibility and light winds. However, the fly in the ointment was a weather warning of thunderstorms and heavy rain. This would be building from around 1000Z and would continue all afternoon, but the Met Office assessed it had only a 30 per cent probability of bringing the weather down temporarily to 4 kilometres visibility in a thunderstorm. This was a very different scenario to London. We assessed the overall picture and in discussion with the forecasters and the SRO, Air Vice Marshal Mayhew, decided that it was worth launching the aircraft – the probability was weighted in our favour that it would be OK. The decision to launch was made. Aircraft serviceability remained high, an outstanding effort by the squadron's engineers, and at the appropriate check-in time, we had everyone airborne and ready in their holds. The weather where the aircraft currently were was fine, my concerns about holding the aircraft over mid-eastern Wales abated as their weather was better than Fairford. However, our concerns over weather were not completely removed. It became tense in our command cell about thirty minutes prior to the scheduled 1315Z overflight. We knew that thunderstorms were a very real possibility. We had been assured, however, that they would be sporadic, short in duration and would clear any particular area quickly. I was quietly confident we would be fine.

The Fairford displays were continuing and the time approached for the Battle of Britain Memorial Flight to start-up. They taxied and were lined up ready for departure.

We had previously given a 'Go' at 1230Z based on the latest weather report but there was something that just didn't feel right. Looking out of the window, which faced due north from where I sat, there were clouds but nothing that was particularly threatening. It looked fine. The aircraft were to approach from the north – they would be able to get here. Maybe it was the slight reduction in light, I'm not really sure. But something prompted me to go outside again and take a 'real-world' look. And I'm glad I did. Directly south-west of the airfield I saw a huge cell of thunderstorm activity. It was very dark grey, looked menacing and was evidently heading our way. The cloud appeared to reach all the way to the ground; the visibility there appeared definitely below our required 5 kilometres. Racing back inside, I grabbed the phone to the Met Office as well as the SRO, as it would be him who would make the Abort call if necessary. AVM Mayhew had also seen the problem and had been in and out of the VIP tents answering questions over the weather, attempting to manage expectations and keeping a close eye on the now deteriorating weather situation. In my other ear I put my mobile phone headphone with a direct line to Swanwick who were speaking to all of the aircraft. It was approaching the time aircraft would start to leave the hold and we would need to make a very rapid decision. The Typhoons would depart the hold at 1303Z with the leading helicopter aircraft overhead at 1315Z. We had a few minutes but nothing more. In times like this, however, it felt like no time at all. We knew that the hold locations were fit. Right now, the actual flypast location of Fairford was fit and, based on the weather data, it would probably remain fit for the flypast. But the egress.... The critical area where aircraft would split apart, climb and return back to their bases looked horrendous. Stood next to the Met Office radar screen, the SRO and I saw a rainbow of colours on the computer. This was not a good sign. It indicated the severity and density of the cloud and rain. Embedded within that was the thunderstorm activity – the 30 per cent chance was looking more like 100 per cent. Would it pass sufficiently to the south or not? Would the decision be made to cancel the flypast for it then to actually all be OK? The thunderstorm cell was definitely moving and it wasn't totally off the cards yet. We had an option. The flypast could be delayed. I looked to the SRO for his decision. Having taken all aspects into account, and taken the decision to the wire, the aircraft were told to hold and having briefed them that there would be no ROLEX (the code-word for a time delay) one was issued.

This was a safe, albeit unbriefed call. We knew the Typhoons were short on fuel and could only hold for a maximum of about ten minutes and we had given ten minutes as the time delay. The Memorial Flight fighters on the ground had radioed in that their engines were starting to overheat. The airshow organisers could accommodate the delay. We had ten minutes. The weather was not abating. A couple of spots of rain started to fall on the airfield. I couldn't really believe it. After the summer heatwave we had had and the parched grass which lay in front of me, it was unbelievable that of all the times to have really poor weather it would be now. I felt incredibly uneasy and over my flying career I've learnt to acknowledge and trust my instincts. There is a phrase in the military and aviation world called 'press-on-itus'. It has sealed the fate of many an intrepid aviator in the past. After more discussions with the forecaster, I voiced my concerns to the SRO that I thought the flypast should be cancelled. With his years of flying experience, and being Air Officer Commanding / SRO for multiple large flypasts over the past three years, his decision had already been made. He was not going to jeopardise the safety of the flypast – the consequences were obvious. The Abort code-word, the one word we had hoped would not have to be used, was sent through to Swanwick. The Fairford flypast was over.

It was a real feeling of dejection. The planning, the paperwork, the enormous effort by all was scuppered by one, inappropriately placed and very badly timed thunderstorm. To make matters worse, I'm pretty sure it was the only one I had seen all summer-long. Fairford did receive spots of rain as the northern edge of the thunderstorm touched the airfield. At the expected time when the aircraft would have been overhead, we knew the right decision had been made. It would have been dangerous to allow the flypast to go ahead. The towering clouds of a cumulonimbus thunderstorm was still very much in full swing immediately to the south. The egress routing on the scale we had, had been intricately planned to ensure all formations deconflicted safely. The formation leaders would have had to make it up on the hoof if they were to avoid the thunderstorm and its very size meant that was probably not possible – at least not safely. As per the Met Office forecast, it was indeed isolated, sporadic and moved through quickly. But that isolated, sporadic thunderstorm was in exactly the wrong place. Frustratingly, twenty minutes later it was all clear. Dejected but vindicated, ultimately the safe and correct decision had been made.

## *Chapter 9*

# Aftermath

The culmination of the big day itself, 10 July 2018, was climactic, but I had very mixed feelings compared to those I had envisaged. This surprised me. The feeling which settled over me was that it really had been about the journey as much as the actual day itself. Don't get me wrong – it was an incredible day and I felt very emotional. I would miss it; I would miss the focus and drive on this project that had been part of my life for the past eighteen months. As I stood watching the final aircraft fly past and the smoke of the Red Arrows disappear in the wind, I reflected on the previous eighteen months and thought about the multitude of video conferences, face-to-face meetings, phone calls, planning sessions, papers and briefings and realised that I relished those aspects as much as seeing the final result. It had been quite a journey in bringing together a plan which started as ideas on a PowerPoint slide and had manifested itself into a national event watched globally. Strangely, it made me think more about life in general. We often get so focused on achieving the end result that we miss the true joys of the task that are generated daily. Of course, there were plenty of challenges, and ups and downs. But now it was over, although not conscious at the time, I realised that I had very much enjoyed the journey; I had fully embraced its ups and its downs. This particular journey, like many, only ever happen once. I think it was this understanding which made me feel surprisingly sad.

That journey of course was made so much more enjoyable by the people that were around me. The key to much that is successful relies on the team that are part of bringing it all to life. I will be truly grateful. There is no way this event could have been successful without everyone who took part. Those key people have been mentioned throughout this book, and of course it would be remiss not to note all those who took part on the day, both airborne and on the ground. The aircraft would not be up there without the engineers, nor been safely manoeuvred around the sky without Air Traffic Control. Everyone had their very important part to play. Throughout the planning phases and the expert advice, opinions and of course the differences that come through an engaged team ensured its success. Failure was not an option. This really was a team effort. Outside the obvious differences when it comes to war-fighting, I don't think that we are markedly different in the military when it comes to genuine teamwork. Much in the civilian sector is the same so there is an obvious read across, but being surrounded by experts who were also as driven to make this a success made the journey less complex and generally far more pleasurable. Of course, we had our differences in opinion and I enjoyed listening to them – my thoughts were often adapted by the discussion and I'm always keen to learn and understand things better. Author and speaker Simon Sinek has said that it is a good leadership trait that leaders speak last. It allows thoughts and ideas to flow to the surface, allows everyone's opinion to be heard and leads to the formation of better judgement. I was consciously aware of this and tried to use this as much as possible. This process also aligns and enhances the 'Mission Command' principle that we try to use in the military. Mission Command essentially allows subordinates to progress a path with as much freedom as possible within given boundaries. It is what allows soldiers, sailors and airmen to use their judgement relatively freely while staying within legal and mission boundaries. It does not abdicate responsibility from above, nor allow someone to go off half-cocked, but provides the maximum degree of freedom to achieve the aim within boundaries. It can sometimes be more difficult to control. With driven people with differing viewpoints and ideas, there is always the danger that the project's path can be altered. It's why abdication cannot work, unless you care little of the outcome. The outcome could end up being so different to what you desire. But by giving ownership to a role or task you also allow people to perform at their best, and they often will gift ideas far better than your own. It is therefore incredibly effective when used properly. I was lucky. Looking upwards through my hierarchy, Mission Command was very effectively used – it solidified my understanding of myself so I know I work best when I have freedom of manoeuvre; know the boundaries but don't have to request permission for every little thing. I hope that I did the same with my team.

I am conscious that nothing like this will probably ever be done again by the Royal Air Force. The reason, the scale and the complexity are something that are literally a once-in-a-lifetime event. Truly once in a centenary. The Royal Air Force is an increasingly complex, integrated, technologically competent machine. The growth of the RAF into a fifth generation Air Force demonstrates that. While I am in no doubt it will last at least a further one hundred years, it will probably be almost unrecognisable in form by then. I doubt that the spectacle of seeing aircraft flying over Central London will even be a reality in 2118. With advancement in technology, adaptations in aircraft to become unmanned air vehicles and with payloads potentially being able to be delivered by smaller or as yet unimagined systems, the look and feel of a Centenary flypast in 2118 will be indescribably different – if there is such a thing.

An oil painting titled RAF100 A Day to Remember by Tim O'Brien GAvA. The original is displayed in the dining-room of the Royal Air Force Club. For more of his fabulous work, please see www.timobrienart.co.uk (www.timobrienart.co.uk)

# Epilogue

On 31 March 2019, the Tornado GR4, the backbone of the Royal Air Force's strike-attack capability, was retired to be replaced by the capable Typhoon and fifth generation F-35 Lightning aircraft. Both 2018 and 2019 marked incredibly special years for me, not least by being given the opportunity of coordinating and delivering the Centenary Flypast for the world's first independent Air Force but also because my role as the Chief of Staff within the Tornado Force Headquarters also came with the oversight and programme management of much of the celebratory Tornado Force drawdown activities. Both 2018 and the early part of 2019 were extremely busy. We celebrated the end of the Tornado Force with a Hangar Party, formal flypast and Gala Dinner. The final ever sortie flown by the Royal Air Force in the Tornado GR4 (ZA463) was flown on 14 March 2019 by Squadron Leader Ian Dornan MBE and Squadron Leader Steve Beardmore MBE. There were more than a few tearful eyes as these events unfolded. 2019 was also personally special as it was my final year as a Regular officer in the Royal Air Force. Having been fascinated by the Royal Air Force and aviation since a boy I have had an incredibly fortunate career doing something I loved every day. I first flew in a Tornado on 10 February 2003 and had managed to fly on XV(R), 12(B), 617 and 31 Squadrons through my career. Amassing over 2,200 hours on the Tornado during this time, I also had a ground tour working within the Defence Equipment and Support organisation before returning to flying duties with 31 Squadron as a Flight Commander executive officer. My last sortie was on 5 August 2015, where following my time on 31, I had transitioned into the role of Officer Commanding the Tornado Standards Unit. It was a really great time with really great people. Following a year at Staff College in 2015/16 I returned to the Tornado Force finishing my career as the Headquarters Chief of Staff. I had been Tornado GR4 through and through. The work has been varied, challenging, with purpose and meaning. It is something I want to replicate for the next few decades of working life. Since joining the Royal Air Force at just under 19 years old, my time 'in' has flown past, quite literally. There has been much change – this is no different to any other organisation and change must happen. It is always a precursor to growth. I feel very lucky to have been surrounded by so many outstanding people, both professionally and personally. Nothing quite beats the camaraderie of being on a front-line squadron.

The author pictured just prior to flying in a practice event in the '100' formation from RAF Coningsby. The weather could not have been better and we all hoped that it would be replicated on 10 July!

(© *Crown Copyright 2018, Sgt Nik Howe*)

Horse Guards Parade was used to provide a static display of some of the aircraft of the Royal Air Force.
(© *Crown Copyright 2018*)

(*© Crown Copyright 2018, SAC Pippa Fowles*)

(*© Crown Copyright 2018, Sgt Nik Howe*)

I won't get that time on a squadron again, but I do look back with great fondness. Having now also project-managed a further two flypasts – the D–Day 75th celebrations at Portsmouth and the NATO 70th Celebration at Fairford in 2019, the frictions of producing such events are much reduced with experience. They are always different however, and always pose different challenges. It is something I relish and there is nothing better than seeing the results of your work displayed. I am proud to have been of service and done my part.

*Appendices*

# List of Appendices

# The Final Plan

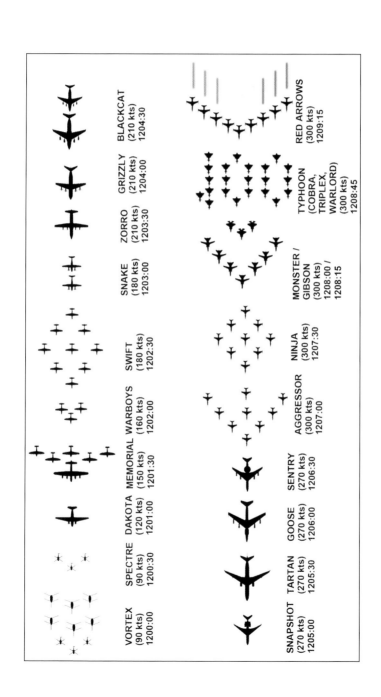

*Appendix II*

# List of Aircraft Participants with Callsign

| | |
|---|---|
| ***Vortex*** | |
| 3 x Puma HC Mk 2 | XW199 |
| | XW217 |
| | ZJ956 |
| 6 x Chinook HC Mk 4/Mk 6 | ZA683 |
| | ZA670 |
| | ZA704 |
| | ZD574 |
| | ZK561 |
| | ZK559 |
| ***Spectre*** | |
| 2 x Juno HT Mk 1 | ZM518 |
| | ZM519 |
| 1 x Jupiter HT Mk 1 | ZM500 |
| ***Dakota*** | |
| 1 x Dakota C Mk 3 | ZA947 |
| ***Memorial*** | |
| 1 x Lancaster B1 | PA474 |
| 3 x Spitfire | MK356 |
| | PS915 |
| | TE311 |
| 2 x Hurricane | LF363 |
| | PZ865 |
| ***Warboys*** | |
| 3 x Prefect T Mk 1 | ZM305 |
| | ZM306 |
| | ZM319 |

*Swift*
9 x Tucano T Mk 1

ZF142
ZF239
ZF287
ZF290
ZF291
ZF348
ZF374
ZF407
ZF512

*Snake*
2 x Shadow R Mk 1

ZZ417
ZZ418

*Zorro*
2 x Hercules C Mk 4 / C Mk 5

ZH868
ZH887

*Grizzly*
1 x Atlas C Mk 1

ZM416

*Blackcat*
1 x C17A Globemaster III
1 x BAe 146 CC Mk 2

ZZ172
ZE700

*Snapshot*
1 x Sentinel R Mk 1

ZJ692

*Tartan*
1 x Voyager KC Mk 2

ZZ330

*Goose*
1 x Rivet Joint RC-135W

ZZ665

*Sentry*
1 x E-3D Sentry AEW Mk 1

ZH103

*Aggressor*
9 x Hawk T Mk 1

XX202
XX205

                                        XX246
                                        XX255
                                        XX303
                                        XX318
                                        XX321
                                        XX348
                                        XX339

*Ninja*
9 x Hawk T Mk 2                          ZK010
                                        ZK012
                                        ZK013
                                        ZK020
                                        ZK025
                                        ZK028
                                        ZK030
                                        ZK031
                                        ZK032

*Monster*
9 x Tornado GR Mk 4                      ZA543
                                        ZA546
                                        ZA585
                                        ZA588
                                        ZA597
                                        ZD792
                                        ZD849
                                        ZG752
                                        ZG775

*Gibson*
3 x Lightning F35-B                      ZM145
                                        ZM147
                                        ZM148

*Typhoon (Warlord, Triplex, Cobra)*
22 x Typhoon FGR Mk 4 / T Mk 3          ZJ802
                                        ZJ916
                                        ZJ920
                                        ZJ939
                                        ZJ942

ZJ950
ZK301
ZK304
ZK306
ZK307
ZK308
ZK310
ZK312
ZK314
ZK316
ZK318
ZK319
ZK320
ZK342
ZK354
ZK357
ZK383

**Red Arrows**
9 x Hawk T Mk 1

XX219
XX278
XX244
XX245
XX310
XX311
XX319
XX322
XX325

*Appendix III*

# List of Participating Departure Airfields

| | |
|---|---|
| RAF Barkston Heath | *Warboys* |
| RAF Brize Norton | *Zorro, Grizzly, Blackcat, Tartan* |
| RAF Coningsby | *Typhoon* |
| RAF Linton-On-Ouse | *Ninja* |
| RAF Marham | *Monster, Gibson* |
| RAF Scampton | *Red Arrows* |
| RAF Waddington | *Snake, Snapshot, Goose, Sentry, Dakota, Memorial* |
| RAF Wattisham | *Swift* |
| RAF Wittering | *Aggressor* |
| Stapleford (civilian) | *Vortex, Spectre* |

# List of Participating Recovery Airfields

| | |
|---|---|
| RAF Barkston Heath | *Warboys* |
| RAF Benson | *Vortex, Spectre, Red Arrows* |
| RAF Boscombe Down | *Aggressor* |
| RAF Brize Norton | *Zorro, Grizzly, Blackcat 1, Tartan* |
| RAF Coningsby | *Typhoon* |
| RAF Fairford | *Dakota, Memorial* (Lancaster) |
| RAF Linton-On-Ouse | *Swift* |
| RAF Marham | *Monster, Gibson* |
| RAF Northolt | *Blackcat 2* |
| RAF Odiham | *Vortex, Ninja* |
| RAF Waddington | *Snake, Snapshot, Goose, Sentry* |
| Southampton (civilian) | *Memorial* (fighters) |

*Note: Cambridge was originally planned to be used, but due to last minute changes with the BBMF, Waddington replaced Cambridge in the final stages.*

*Appendix V*

# The Weather Options

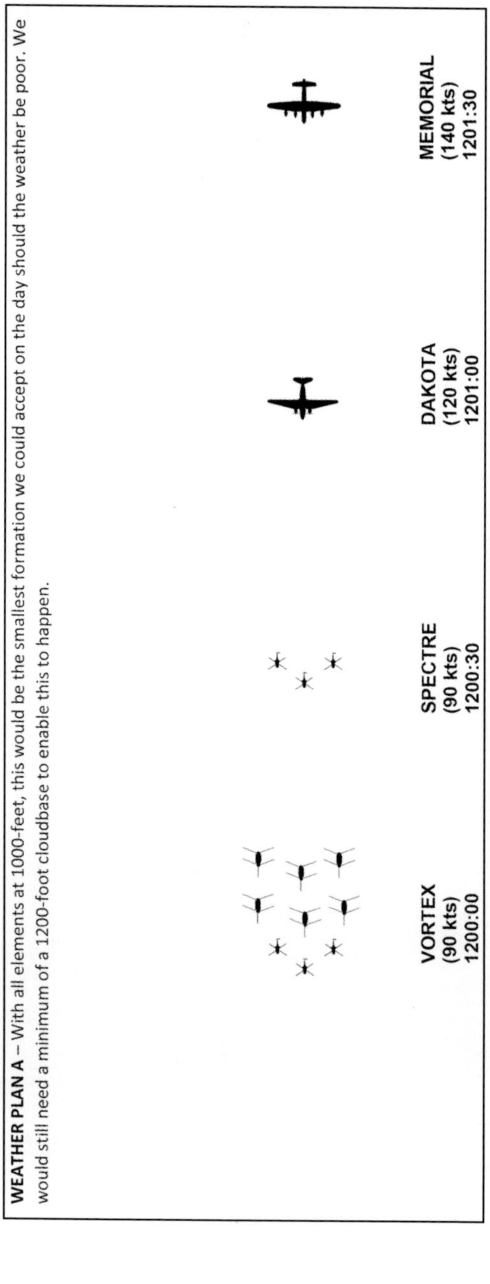
WEATHER PLAN A – With all elements at 1000-feet, this would be the smallest formation we could accept on the day should the weather be poor. We would still need a minimum of a 1200-foot cloudbase to enable this to happen.
VORTEX
(90 kts)
1200:00
SPECTRE
(90 kts)
1200:30
DAKOTA
(120 kts)
1201:00
MEMORIAL
(140 kts)
1201:30

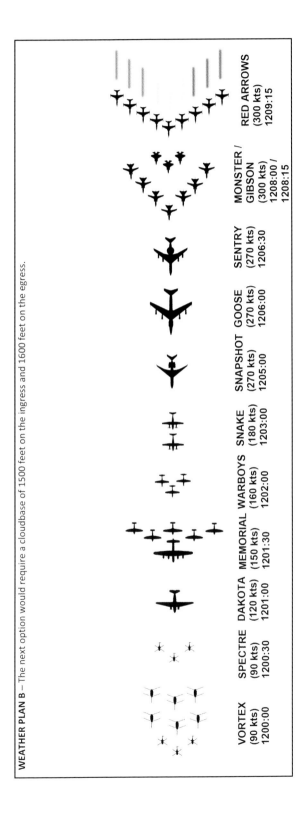

WEATHER PLAN B – The next option would require a cloudbase of 1500 feet on the ingress and 1600 feet on the egress.

| VORTEX | SPECTRE | DAKOTA | MEMORIAL | WARBOYS | SNAKE | SNAPSHOT | GOOSE | SENTRY | MONSTER / | RED ARROWS |
| (90 kts) | (90 kts) | (120 kts) | (150 kts) | (160 kts) | (180 kts) | (270 kts) | (270 kts) | (270 kts) | GIBSON | (300 kts) |
| 1200:00 | 1200:30 | 1201:00 | 1201:30 | 1202:00 | 1203:00 | 1205:00 | 1206:00 | 1206:30 | (300 kts) | 1209:15 |
| | | | | | | | | | 1208:00 / | |
| | | | | | | | | | 1208:15 | |

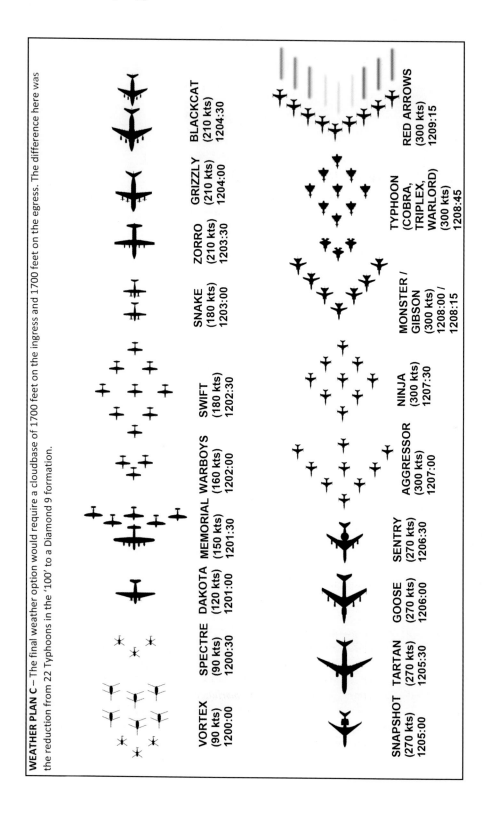

**WEATHER PLAN C** – The final weather option would require a cloudbase of 1700 feet on the ingress and 1700 feet on the egress. The difference here was the reduction from 22 Typhoons in the '100' to a Diamond 9 formation.

VORTEX
(90 kts)
1200:00

SPECTRE
(90 kts)
1200:30

DAKOTA
(120 kts)
1201:00

MEMORIAL
(150 kts)
1201:30

WARBOYS
(160 kts)
1202:00

SWIFT
(180 kts)
1202:30

SNAKE
(180 kts)
1203:00

ZORRO
(210 kts)
1203:30

GRIZZLY
(210 kts)
1204:00

BLACKCAT
(210 kts)
1204:30

SNAPSHOT
(270 kts)
1205:00

TARTAN
(270 kts)
1205:30

GOOSE
(270 kts)
1206:00

SENTRY
(270 kts)
1206:30

AGGRESSOR
(300 kts)
1207:00

NINJA
(300 kts)
1207:30

MONSTER /
GIBSON
(300 kts)
1208:00 /
1208:15

TYPHOON
(COBRA,
TRIPLEX,
WARLORD)
(300 kts)
1208:45

RED ARROWS
(300 kts)
1209:15

*Appendix VI*

# RAF 100 Insignia

### Appendix F – RAF 100 Flying Suit Patches

A superb idea from one of the team was to make a set of patches (along with other memorabilia) that could be worn by the aircrew on the main events of the flypast. They would also serve as a treasured memory for years to come. Kindly reproduced with the permission of Squadron Prints, (www.squadronprints.co.uk), Gill and Berry Vissers produced the designs as you can see below.

*Above left*: *Vortex*. The lead formation of the RAF 100 Flypast. The formation consisted of three Puma and six Chinook aircraft from RAF Benson and RAF Odiham.

*Above middle*: *Spectre*. The second helicopter formation consisting of one Jupiter and two Juno aircraft. The newest helicopter additions to the Defence Helicopter Flying School based at RAF Shawbury.

*Above right*: *Dakota* and *Memorial*. A circular patch for the Battle of Britain Memorial Flight showing both the BBMF formations of *Dakota* and *Memorial*. Note that in the formation of *Memorial*, production is different on the patch to that which was subsequently flown. The challenges of fighter serviceability and qualified pilots to fly them meant the final formation constitution was subtly different to that which was submitted on the patch design.

*Above left*: *Warboys*. A further display of the RAF's newest training aircraft to enter the fleet came in the form of three Prefect aircraft. Under No. 3 Elementary Flying School, the Prefect is flown in the first stage of pilot training.

*Above middle*: *Swift*. A formation of nine Tucano aircraft based at RAF Linton-On-Ouse. The Tucano has been in RAF service for more than twenty-five years. The aircraft type subsequently went out of service in late 2019.

*Above right*: *Snake*. Always in high demand and operating in the Intelligence, Surveillance and Reconnaissance role, we were fortunate to be able to showcase two Shadow aircraft operated by 14 Squadron from RAF Waddington.

*Above left*: *Zorro*. The main formation that was originally planned was for just one Hercules aircraft. A back-up option for numbers was for an additional Hercules to be flown in line astern. The patch represented the original plan rather than the contingency option – which was subsequently used!

*Above middle*: *Grizzly*. The Atlas followed the Hercules formation. Originally, we wanted up to four of these aircraft in formation but due to availability, only one could be guaranteed.

*Above right*: *Blackcat*. An unusual combination of a C17 Globemaster and BAe 146. Operated by 99 Squadron and 32 (The Royal) Squadron respectively from RAF Brize Norton and RAF Northolt.

*Above left*: *Snapshot*. An unusual sight to see so low over London. The Sentinel aircraft operated from V(AC) Squadron was a fantastic addition to the flypast and showcased another of the RAF's surveillance aircraft.

*Above middle*: *Tartan*. The RAF's largest aircraft is the Voyager. Operating in a passenger, cargo carrying and air-air refuelling role, the aircraft is certainly versatile. The Voyager entered service in 2011 replacing the venerable fleet of VC-10s and Tristars.

*Above right*: *Goose*. Another aircraft seldomly seen, unless watching it take off and land from its base at RAF Waddington, was the Rivet Joint aircraft. This is operated by 51 Squadron and delivers battle-winning signals intelligence information to commanders on the ground.

*Above left*: *Sentry*. The instantly recognisable AWACS aircraft was the final 'heavy' aircraft in the RAF 100 formation. Operated by 8 Squadron from RAF Waddington, this aircraft has long been the RAF's Airborne Early Warning aircraft.

*Above middle*: *Aggressor*. The 100 Squadron Hawks from RAF Leeming led the fast-jet formations of the flypast.

*Above right*: *Ninja*. Following the Hawk T Mark 1 were the Diamond Nine formation of the new Hawk T Mark 2 aircraft from IV Squadron based at RAF Valley.

*Above left: Monster.* Flying in their last major flypast, the Tornado formation was originally meant to be just seven aircraft as per the patch design. A contingency option of the additional two aircraft was flown on the day as well slightly astern the main formation. The overall formation lead of *Windsor Formation* was in *Monster 1.*

*Above middle: Gibson.* The historic 617 Squadron fly the latest aircraft to join the RAF. We were fortunate to have three F-35 Lightning II aircraft in the flypast as they had only recently arrived from the United States. The Lightning is without doubt the most technologically advanced aircraft the RAF has ever operated.

*Above right: Typhoon (Warlord, Triplex, Cobra).* The spectacle of the formation was the '100' flown by the Typhoon Force. Consisting of a total of twenty-two aircraft from RAF Coningsby and RAF Lossiemouth, the Typhoon Force was the only Force to be able to field this many aircraft in one go. Simply spectacular!

*Red Arrows.* The iconic Royal Air Force Aerobatic Team concluded the flypast with their traditional Red, White and Blue smoke. Always a crowd-pleaser. Their patch had to be grey to ensure the red aircraft and smoke were visible.

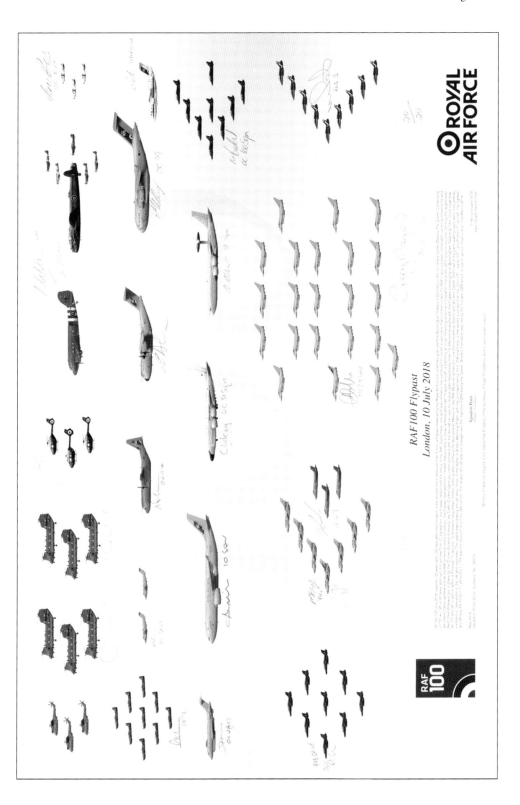

RAF 100 Flypast
London, 10 July 2018

# Index